The Wisdom Within

A GUIDE TO THE TARA WISDOM CARDS

JESSICA ZEBRINE

FOREWORD BY

PREMA DASARA

Acknowledgments

I am filled with gratitude for Tara, the Great Mother Protector who inspires this work. All mistakes are mine. All praise is Hers.

Thank you, Prema, who brought Tara into my life through your teachings.

www.TaraWisdomCards.com

Foreword by Prema Dasara

The Wisdom Ways call us to manifest our highest potential. As human beings possessing sentience, consciousness, and awareness, we have extraordinary possibilities. Legends and myths, even current stories, tell us of human beings who demonstrated profound abilities to love, to heal, to humor, to nurture, to inspire, and to uplift.

When we determine that we want to bring to fulfillment this potential, we turn to those who have gone before to show us the path. It is at once a solitary journey and one in which we take the entire world with us. For we are interconnected with all that exists, and yet we also hold a unique position in this magnificent ever changing tapestry. This self-awareness is where the journey with the 21 Taras and the Major Arcana of the Tarot begins.

Having lived and breathed the 21 Praises of Tara since 1986, this book is my small contribution to the incredible practices and teachings that are assembled around the magnificent being we call Tara. Mother of the Universe, Mother of All Buddhas, Mother Earth (Terra), Mother of

Wisdom, this divine feminine presence has made Herself known on this planet in a myriad of ways.

She has appeared to people visibly in a corporeal body to save them from disaster, to encourage them to reach for their highest aspiration. She has appeared in a body of light to countless people guiding them. She appears within dreams, she promises to guide us at the moment of death. She vowed to remain in the body of a woman until the end of time, saving beings from the endless frustrations of a life lived in ignorance, aggression, and desire.

I believe the Tarot was born from the inspiration of Her Praises. Certainly they come from the same esoteric source. Both bodies of inspiration have been adopted by countless aspirants, yogis, and magi, seeking to communicate to the ones following in their footsteps the means to be free from confusion and to manifest all enlightened qualities.

One line of speculation about the cards is that they were developed by magi as a way to preserve eternal truths in a mundane form that would escape the eye of the church, which was actively destroying any spiritual expression that threatened its supremacy. The cards appeared innocuous, only an initiate would understand the wisdom they represented.

Having received teachings, empowerments and transmission from many of the greatest Lamas of our time you will see some of their touch on these pages. But for the most part you will find a western lay woman encountering two profound paths....the wisdom of Tibetan Buddhism and the Wisdom of the Western mystery schools, influenced by the Kabala, the alchemists, the Theosophists... great thinkers, great hearts. On the path of wisdom as soon as you have some realization, you reach out your hand to those following, knowing how difficult the journey can be. This book allows us to walk together, exploring how these two sets of revelation inform and augment each other.

The key to both are the symbols that inform each card, each Tara. It was through the symbols that I recognized how uncanny the relationships are. Jung tells us that in order to truly penetrate the subconscious, the storehouse of our experience throughout time and space, we can ride on the powerful religious symbols of our times. The Tibetans say the idealized forms of the deities act like keys to our subconscious. Jung said the archetypes will take us into the depths. This is the main aspect of this exploration. These teachings arose for me through the medium of dance and song. The sacred arts are designed to drive us into the deepest part of our being if we open to them.

My niece, Jessica Zebrine, was inspired by this transmission, and through her own practice and profound educational opportunities, she has shaped these Tara Wisdom Cards. Using them herself over decades she has gained insight into key words that express the symbolic power.

The mind offers its profound insight when it is open and stimulated. Using these cards is an excellent method of moving beyond the intellectual capacity of the mind into the deep well of insight. Select one card, and let its symbolic wisdom stimulate your deep mind. Enjoy the insight that arises.

Come. Open your heart and your mind.

- Prema Dasara, April 18, 2016

Preface to the 2nd Edition By Jessica Zebrine

As I write this, we are just beginning to dance again in larger groups for the first time since the global pandemic of the coronavirus. I don't know anyone who has not personally been affected. Many have chosen not to return to the life they had before, but they are still seeking answers. The cards are a good way to find the windows and doors into the dharma.

In the six years since I published the deck, I have had the opportunity to refine the techniques of reading. I've read cards on three continents now, and for people all over the world through Zoom. I especially loved participating in the Tara Monlam in Brazil in 2018 and sharing with so many dancers while I was there.

I often feel like I am reading for myself any time I read for someone else. Tara tells me exactly what I need to hear. I have made some beautiful connections reading for others. I'd love to read cards more, so if you're ever interested in getting a reading, feel free to schedule one through zoom:

https://linktr.ee/Irisimaginoria

I also discovered new ways to read the cards. I still use the original spread I created based on the dance, the birth card with the triangle, etc. But quite often I will use a "rainbow chakra" spread. I also developed a set of lithomancy Tara stones that I use in conjunction with the cards. I will include information about all of these in the opening section of this second edition book.

I wish you many blessings as you find what you will find in these pages. Om Tare!

Introduction by Jessica Zebrine

All my life I knew my mother's sister was beautiful and exotic, a dancer in India and Hawaii, and completely out of reach. We had a photo of her in the hallway, and occasionally we got small cards or notes, but mostly she was a myth. Even her name, Prema Dasara, was unusual and mysterious. I felt a longing for a spiritual connection with someone from my family, from my roots, so I sent a heartfelt plea to a stranger's E-mail, and through cyberspace I formed one of the deepest connections in my life. Then Prema introduced me to practices and a mythos that would inform every part of my belief system.

Why are we here? What is our great purpose on the planet? I strongly believe we are here to bring benefit to the world, and we do that by manifesting the wisdom, compassion, and power that we already have within. This is the core of the practices of Tara, Tibetan Buddha Goddess of Wisdom, Compassion, and Power. We each have all of the qualities of the Buddhas and Bodhisattvas inside, and through practice and purifications, we can manifest them through an enlightened state.

The Tara Wisdom Cards are based on the lineage tradition of the "The Mandala Dance of the 21 Praises of Tara." This dance meditation practice was developed by my aunt Prema with the guidance of several Tibetan teachers. The Tara Dance has been performed by thousands of women of all ages, nationalities, and walks of life. Prema's organization, Tara Dhatu (www.taradhatu.net), empowers and uplifts through the sacred arts.

Prema discovered a correlation between the many forms of Tara and the imagery of the 21 major arcana of the tarot. After attending her Tara & Tarot workshop, I began the project of creating the Tara Wisdom Cards in 2003. I began with the 22 major arcana. I learned tarot through this project, exploring the traditional Buddhist images and how they could correlate with the meanings of traditional tarot cards. Then I worked on the minor arcana, comparing the traditional meanings to the dharma teachings.

At the time I was just learning to use Photoshop, self-publishing was rare, and crowdfunding did not exist. For years I searched for a better artist to bring my vision into reality. In 2014, while recovering from breast cancer, I discovered that the artist I sought was inside me already. With 11 years of Photoshop experience, more opportunities for self-publishing, and a successful Kickstarter campaign, I was able to realize my dream with the production of 1,000 decks.

The cards were born out of years of study, practice, meditation, and divination. The 22 Tara images themselves were drawn and painted digitally by me based on the line drawings of the Suryagupta traditional images of Tara found in Bokar Rinpoche's book *Tara: The Feminine Divine*. There are many, many color variations in different traditions. I primarily used the colors for each Tara from the Mandala Dance tradition, though for most I chose secondary and supplemental colors. I learned meanings behind the many different Buddhist symbols and ritual objects in the images.

For the minor arcana, I relied more closely on my experiences of the four elements in modern Paganism. My elemental interpretations are a blend between the Tibetan and Western elemental traditions.

The deck can be used for meditation or as a divinatory system. Divination is opening to the messages of the Divine. Anyone can read cards for divination. Just look at the images and let them tell you a story. Trust yourself. The pages of this book will help explain some of the symbolism of the cards, but the most significant reading will come from your own interpretation.

The Tara Wisdom Cards are a tool for experiencing the dharma and finding your own glimpses of enlightenment. The images are like windows and doors to let the dharma come through.

WHO IS TARA?

This unique deck of cards is based on the many faces and forms of Tara, the Tibetan Buddha Goddess of Wisdom, Compassion and Power. In Her legend, Tara was an ordinary woman who practiced the dharma and attained enlightenment. Before entering the Awakened State she vowed to remain in the form of a woman until the end of time to free all beings from suffering.

The dharma teaches that we have all the qualities of an enlightened being latent within us. We can learn from Tara about our own true wisdom nature.

COLORS OF TARA

Tara arises through a vibration of sound and light. The color (vibration of light) of each Tara is significant. Tara manifests in five basic colors (vibration of light), which represent the colors of the five Wisdom "families." Some Taras manifest in a combination of colors and meaning. TAM (pronounced tahm) is Tara's seed syllable. This illustration is the Tibetan letter of TAM.

Green Tara: Enlightened Activity

White Tara: Peace and Spaciousness

Gold Tara: Abundance and Good Fortune

Red Tara: Magnetism and Power

Blue Tara: Discipline and Precision

~

TARA'S MANTRA:

OM TARE TUTARE TURE SOHA

A mantra is a string of sacred syllables that invokes the power of an Enlightened Being. Tara's mantra means:

OM: All that exists.
TARE: Great Mother
TUTARE: Remover of fears and obstacles
TURE: Bestower of good fortune
SOHA: So it is

~

PRAYER OF MOTIVATION

The purpose of Tara meditations and practices is to bring benefit to all beings. When I give a Tara Wisdom Cards reading, I begin with this prayer, written by Prema:

We are here to manifest
the wisdom that rests within.

We are here to radiate
our loving compassion
into the world.

We are here to gather
the skill and the power
to bless and empower all.

MANDALA READING LAYOUT:

For a full reading, I lay out the cards in the pattern of the full 22 dancer Mandala and spiral out from the center telling the story.

After having a person shuffle or cut the cards, I begin with the center card, the birth card. This is the aspect of Tara that is being born right now in a person's life. It can be the first card I pull from the deck, or I could calculate the birth card according to the numerology of a person's date of birth. Add each digit of month, day, and year. If the sum is 21 or less, the corresponding Major Arcana Tara is the person's "birth card." If not, add the two digits. The number of this sum is the person's birth card. For example, the birth of 04/27/1977 would be:

4+2+7+1+9+7+7= 37

3+7 = 10

Birth Card = Tara #10, Joy and Laughter

THE TRIANGLE:

Spiraling out from the center (in the direction shown here), the next step is the triangle, representing body, mind, and speech (or spirit). These are often called the three "gateways" or "mysteries." These three aspects of self are fundamental to the path to enlightenment.

THE INNER CIRCLE:

The inner circle of six cards represents the closer aspects of their life (friends, family, close relationships).

THE OUTER CIRCLE:

The outer circle, which represents the outside influences in a person's life (work, acquaintances, etc). How does this person meet the world?

ADAPTATIONS:

A shorter reading would just include the ten cards of the center, triangle, and inner circle (see illustration). A four-card reading would be the triangle and center. I've had much success with this system of card reading.

RAINBOW CHAKRA BRIDGE READING

The rainbow chakra bridge layout also gives quite effective readings with this deck as it spans both material and abstract planes quite comprehensively. I choose seven cards and consider them according to the seven chakras:

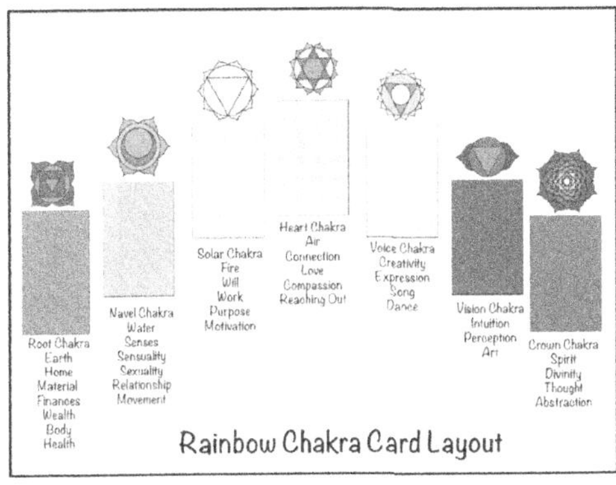

Root Chakra: Earth, Home, Material, Finances, Wealth, Body, Health.

Navel Chakra: Water, Senses, Sensuality, Sexuality, Relationship, Movement.

Solar Chakra: Fire, Will, Work, Purpose, Motivation.

Heart Chakra: Air, Connection, Love, Compassion, Reaching Out.

Voice Chakra: Creativity, Expression, Song, Dance.

Vision Chakra: Intuition, Perception, Art

Crown Chakra: Spirit, Divinity, Thought, Abstraction.

LITHOMANCY

Some of my earliest magical practices were with gemstones. I found I had an affinity for stones right away. I love the practical nature of color and the touch. I also found that gemstones radiate Tara strongly, for each stone shines a radiance of color and light. Opaque stones have a very different presence than translucent stones of the same color, for example. I chose a set of twenty-two stones to correspond with the twenty-two major arcana Taras and keep them in a bag with my deck. When I give a reading, I will ask the person I am reading for to choose stones to go along with the cards. I can them make correlations between the stones and the cards. Sometimes the stones are just used to answer additional questions or like boosters. Sometimes I have the person I'm reading hold the stone during the reading. I will include each stone with its card as I explain the major arcana.

REVERSED CARDS:

In traditional Tarot readings, when a card appears upside down, its meaning is reversed. A negative card would be positive and vice versa. I, personally, do not use reversed cards in my readings. If a card is upside down, I simply turn it upright. If you wish to work with reversed meanings, by all means do. I will be focusing on the upright meanings in this commentary.

CLOSING PRAYER OF BENEFIT:

I always close my readings by unwinding the mandala (picking up the cards mindfully in reverse order from how I laid them down), and then I offer this prayer, which is similar to the closing prayer of benefit that we do in the Tara dances:

Whatever power or knowledge
we achieve through this sincere practice,
may it be for the benefit of all. Svaha. Soha.

Major Arcana: The 21 Praises of Tara

"The 21 Praises of Tara" is a very popular chant within Tibetan Buddhism. The text begins with an elaboration on Tara's mantra

"OM TARE TUTARE TURE SOHA."

This is also often called the "root mantra," and it can be interpreted as a description of all of Her aspects combined, the central Tara. In addition to this central aspect, the 21 Praises of Tara honor 21 specific aspects of Tara.

There are several different versions of the text, particularly as it is translated into English. The Major Arcana of the Tara Wisdom Cards and the Praises listed here are based on an adaptation by Jeff Munoz and Prema Dasara (©1985), a translation specifically intended for singing and dancing. This is the version used in the Tara Mandala Dance (http://www.taradhatu.org).

For each manifestation of Tara and major arcana card, I will describe the image, color, background imagery, and my interpretation of connection to the traditional tarot.

Then Prema offers commentary about each Tara based on her many years of practice and teaching. She compares each to the tarot cards of the well-known Rider-Waite deck.[1]

There is great significance to each Tara's colors, implements or tools, items of jewelry, and mudras (hand gestures). Each wears:

- A crown with five wisdom jewels, representing the five Buddha families,
- A topknot representing highest mind and flowing hair for freedom,
- Earrings and at least two necklaces (one short for mindfulness and one long for joy).

In many of Her images she is seated on a moon cushion with a moon halo, though some are standing and some have fire in place of the moon. Each Tara is sitting or standing on a lotus, for she is the lotus-born one.

#0: Wisdom, Compassion & Power

Tarot Archetype:
The Fool
(Beginnings, innocence, spontaneity, a free spirit)

Tara #0 Praise:

Om All Praises
To The Venerable Exalted Tara
Praise Her Tare,
Liberator Swift and Courageous
Through Tutare Remover of All Fears
Through Ture Bestower of Good Fortune
Through Soha The World Bows at Her Feet

This card features the Central Tara of **Wisdom, Compassion and Power**. She corresponds to the traditional tarot archetype of the fool, the innocent who is open to anything and represents unity.

She is Green Tara. Her body is a luminous green, like a meadow in springtime. Her left hand is in the **mudra of perfect refuge** at Her heart, while Her right hand reaches out in the **mudra of perfect giving**.

Her left leg is pulled in, for she has mastered the power of desire, and Her right leg is extended, for she is quick to go to all who call out to Her.

She has five gems in Her crown, representing the five Buddhas and five states of being. Her short necklace represents mindfulness and Her long necklace represents joy. She is covered with a rainbow of scarves, for she is willing to draw others to Her to bring them benefit.

In Her left she holds the stem of a blue lotus, for she rises above samsara existence just as a lotus is born out of the fertile muck and mire of the world. A moon shines behind Her head, and Her cushion is the moon. She is connected to the impermanent changing moon, as well as the feminine mysteries. She is seated on a purple lotus, a manifestation of spirit, and another lotus springs from Her outstretched foot.

The background of the card shows an infinite blue sky as expansive as the mind, and a brilliant rainbow, symbolizing the wholeness of Tara's many aspects, for she reflects all aspects of light, the full spectrum of life.

The number, 0, represents emptiness and completeness. The number is accented by an image of our world, symbolizing Tara's willingness to meet us in our own realm of understanding. The world is located beneath Her foot, as "The World Bows at Her Feet." She represents infinite possibilities, just as the Fool in the traditional tarot is ready to face anything. The Fool is the protagonist of our story, taking us through the great mysteries of life. The central Tara is the connection between all things.

The lithomancy stone to correspond with Tara #0: **Chrysocolla & Azurite**, a stone that looks like the world itself.

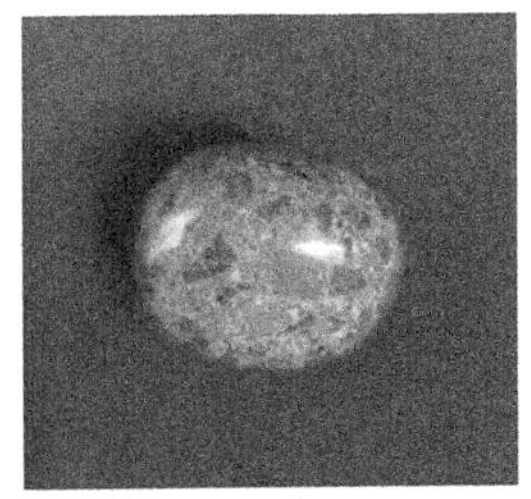

PREMA'S COMMENTARY

In the beginning there was nothing, no thing, no isolation, no separation. Sea of becoming, ocean of consciousness, no beginning, no end. Referred to as emptiness, as ultimate mind. This is the pool out of which Tara arises. Her essential qualities of wisdom, compassion, and great power.

It is said that all we have to do is call out Her name and she is with us, in a blink of an eye, in an instant. This is Tara arising into form, Tara carrying all potential, all enlightened qualities.

All 21 Praises radiate out from this central arising, this zero point. This first gesture of praise towards Tara is actually not included in the 21 Taras classically. It is part of this particular practice, and it allows us to show the relationship of the 21 Taras and the major Arcana of the Tarot. For there we also have the zero and the 21.

Zero, represented by the Fool, possessing everything that is needed for the journey of manifesting the fullness of consciousness, willing to move through every step, every condition, every circumstance, to gather the information and the skill in order to fully integrate all of mind's possibilities.

#1: Swift Protection

Tarot Archetype:
The Magician
(Power, skill, concentration, action, resourcefulness)

Tara #1 Praise:

Praise Her, Protectress,
The Swift and Courageous Tara
Whose Look Is Like
a Flash of Lightning.
Tara Appeared From
An Open Lotus Flower
Born from A Tear of
the Lord of Compassion

Tara of **Swift Protection** is red. She corresponds in the traditional tarot major arcana to the Magician archetype, who uses various magical tools to channel the essence of power.

She has eight arms. The two center arms she holds above Her head in the mudra of great bliss holding a dorje, which symbolizes lightning and **strength**, and a bell, which represents **impermanence and emptiness**.

In Her other right hands, Tara holds an arrow (**alertness and consciousness**), a dharma wheel (**truth**), and a sword (**destroyer of ignorance**). In Her other left hands she holds a bow (**direction and purpose**), a conch (**glory**), and a rope (**liberation**).

Tara uses all of these tools to bring protection to all who need Her. Her eyes are "like a flash of lightning." A flaming sun radiates behind Her head and beneath Her lotus cushion. The sun is the source of energy in this solar system, the origin from which all power emanates.

It is said that Tara entered our realm when Shakyamuni Buddha cried a pool of tears for those who were suffering. Out of this pool, a lotus grew, and out of the lotus, Tara appeared. She was "Born of a Tear of the Lord of Compassion."

In the background, dramatic lightning fills the sky. Lightning is a direct manifestation of power, yet it comes and goes swiftly, often leaving little evidence in its wake.

So does Tara of Swift Protection arrive and depart in the blink of an eye, subtly changing the world with Her wisdom and power.

When the red Tara of Swift Protection arises in your reading, consider what dangers you might face on your path. How can you protect yourself against suffering and harm? Who else in your life needs protection?

Lightning. Illuminating. Flashes of enlightenment. Power. Focus. The magician. Tools.

The lithomancy stone for this Tara is a **red Tiger's Eye**. The flash can be seen like lightning.

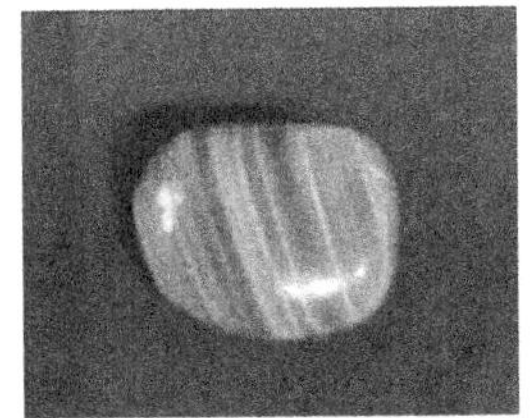

PREMA'S COMMENTARY:

Tara number one, the Swift Protectress. With one we appear in the realm of phenomena, duality arises. In fact, one and zero, that makes two. We are starting to move. And upon what do we move? What is the basis of our movement? The will. She appears swiftly through the tears of the Lord of Compassion. That is one of Her motifs, the swiftness, for she is full action. She is willing to respond to us whenever we call out to Her. In the relationship of Tara number 1 to the Tarot number 1, we have this center point. We are appearing in phenomena. This is the Magician, the "I will." Holding the wand of power, the wand that is able to direct the consciousness, we are arising now into duality.

But how is this to be fruitful? Only if it is in relationship to the unity which is represented by zero, by all that exists, by no separation, and by interconnectedness.

Tara number 1 and the Tarot of number 1 represents this appearance in phenomena. With Her eyes like lightning, this is the symbol that connects us back into the card because the lightning bolt is the wand of power. This is Indra's wand power. When it strikes the earth it brings forth life and fertilizes the earth, for the lightning striking the planet brings about the possibility of creation.

#2: Creative Wisdom

Tarot Archetype:
The High Priestess
(Intuition, higher powers, mystery, subconscious mind)

Tara #2 Praise:

Praise Her the One
Whose Face is Sublimely White
Shining with the Light of
a Hundred Full Autumn Moons.
She Blazes with the Light
of Thousands of Stars
Radiating Light,
Most Excellent and Bright

Tara of **Creative Wisdom** is white with the moon's radiance. She corresponds to the traditional tarot archetype of the High Priestess, who like the moon reflects all wisdom and intention.

She has three faces symbolizing three bodies. Her right face is blue, Her center face is white, and Her left face is golden. Her triplicate nature reflects the impermanent, triplicate nature of the waxing, full and waning moon, as well as the feminine archetypes of maiden, mother and crone.

She has twelve arms symbolizing twelve interdependant factors. Her center hands meet in a mudra of **meditation**.

In Her right hands she holds a garland of marigolds (**praise and honor**), a dorje (**lightning and strength**), a jewel (**granter of wishes**), a dharma wheel (**truth**), and a *khatavanga*, or magic wand (**discipline**).

In Her left hands she holds a text (**transcendental wisdom**), a treasure vase (**abundance**), a bell (**wisdom and impermanence**), a lotus (**purity**) and a water vase (**sacrifice and fulfillment**). These tools are richly colored and varying, as Tara of Creative Wisdom uses Her many resources available to work through various obstacles. She is the mistress of creativity and of the moon, the High Priestess, related to Brigid, Saraswati, etc., and thus is patroness of the arts, theatre, writing, dance, etc. However, Her true creativity is the ability to see multiple perspectives on any problem.

In the background of the card is an image of the Orion nebula. In this cloud, the conditions are optimal for the new stars to be born. Stars are born in clouds of gas under the pull of gravity over eons. As matter is pulled together, it ignites from fusion inside, like creative fires within us. Stars form by balancing the power of the energy inside vs. the gravity outside.

This reflects the magnitude of Tara's creative process, giving birth not only to ideas and art, but also to the very universe itself.

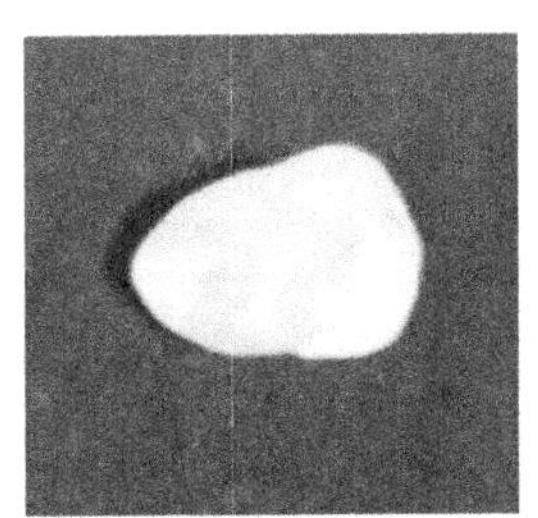

The lithomancy stone for this Tara is **rainbow moonstone**.

A brilliant full moon accents Her number. Tara illuminates all things through the light of Her stars and the moon, the intuitive process of reflection and impermanence.

PREMA'S COMMENTARY:

One cannot exist without two because rising out of the zero, it automatically becomes binary, zero, one, two. Two is implied when one arises. When the point arises, it immediately vibrates. The vibration forward and backward, up and down, in and out.

Tara number two represents Creative Wisdom, that true innate wisdom, that feminine wisdom, that ability to reflect deeply into the interconnectedness of all that exists. Within that deep reflection all interrelationships are revealed. The past informs the present and the future, so we can understand more fully when we see the whole picture.

THE HIGH PRIESTESS.

This is the card of the High Priestess. The motif, the symbol that carries through both card and Tara is the full moon. This Tara is described with the face like the radiance of the full moon, that ultimate reflective aspect that allows us to move deeply into circumstance and see what the interrelationships of all things are. Great art is born from this: seeing the totality, seeing the relationships, and being creative moving into life with this kind of understanding.

This Tara is known as Saraswati, Yang Chen Mo, melodious voice, for she uses all the different aspects of creation in order to reflect back the beauty and wonder of life.

#3: Impeccable Virtue

Tarot Archetype:
The Empress
(Fertility, femininity, beauty, nature, abundance)

Tara #3 Praise:

Praise Her the One with
a Body of Molten Gold
Her Hand Is Adorned With
a Blue Lotus Flower
Engaged in the Six Perfections,
Generous and Virtuous,
Diligent and Peaceful,
Patient and Meditative

Tara of **Impeccable Virtue** brings about fertility and abundance through deep spiritual work. She corresponds to the traditional tarot archetype of the Empress, who also represents fertility and the earth.

She is often described as golden, but in the dance she is green, so she radiates both colors. She is the ripening fields as well as the grain ready for harvest. She sits atop a golden lotus, radiating the power of increase and abundance. She is the fertility of the earth, abundance in all forms.

She has ten arms. In Her center right hand she holds a mala, which represents the complete **cycle of existence**. The cycle of birth, life, death and rebirth reflect the fertility of the earth. Her other right hands hold a sword (**destroyer of ignorance**), an arrow (**alertness and consciousness**), a dorje (**lightning and power**) and a trident (**the three-fold jewel of buddha, dharma and sangha**). In Her left hands she holds a silk scarf (**bless-**

ings), a rope (**liberation**), a lotus (**purity**), a bell (**wisdom and impermanence**) and a bow (**direction**).

She uses these tools to bring forth change and growth, liberation for all beings. A field of ripened wheat emphasizes Her fecund nature, and a laurel wreath shows honor and respect. The seeds you have planted and cultivated are ready to harvest. Her virtues are the six perfections:

- Generosity
- Virtue
- Diligence
- Peacefulness
- Patience
- Meditativeness.

The lithomancy stone for this Tara is the luscious green **malachite** with multiple striations of green.

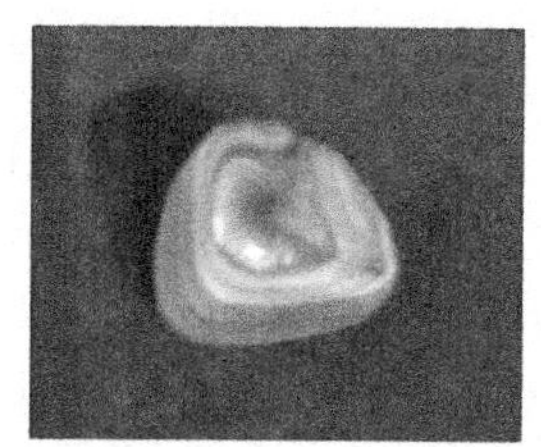

Tara #3 gives you many tools to use in your continued cultivation and harvest of these virtues. Use them wisely. What you sow, you shall reap. You are not expected to be perfect in the perfections, but you have the ability to practice them and bring forth change and growth.

PREMA'S COMMENTARY:

When we combine 1, "I Will," the great masculine, with 2, "I know," the great feminine, then we have the beautiful revelation of the earth and its bounty. Tara number 3, golden body with a cast of green, holds a blue lotus flower for this represents increase, not only the fullness of life, but of our wisdom, of our understanding.

It is said that this Tara represents virtue, but we must understand what virtue means - that which nourishes life. If we are virtuous, we understand the different elements that are needed in order for life to flourish. We also need to understand what is going to inhibit life's flourishing. If we are to move through the world, we must do so in a responsible way, understanding what interrelationship is and what is the result of our action. What holds us back is this misconception of separation, that we are isolated and alone, and in that way we are unstable. In our instability we grasp onto things, places, people, to give us satisfaction. We push away anything that seems to threaten this sense of self or separation and therefore engage in complete confusion.

The reflection into the Tarot, the Empress. Again representing the fullness of life's bounty, the flowering garden. We have united heaven and earth, we have united spirit and matter, and the earth is fertile. The garden is ready.

#4: All Victorious

Tarot Archetype:
The Emperor
(Authority, father-figure, structure, solid foundation)

Tara #4 Praise:

Praise Her Who Sits Above
the Heads of the Buddhas
Enjoying and Abiding in
Complete and Infinite Victory
Those Who Have Mastered,
Achieved the Six Perfections,
The Children of the Enlightened Ones
Deeply Honor Her

All **Victorious** Tara is triumphant over all obstacles. She corresponds to the traditional Tarot archetype of the Emperor, who is the royal monarch, exerting reasoned control over his subjects to bring them benefit.

Tara #4 has achieved the six perfections mentioned in #3's praise. She is victorious over all things.

She is golden with four arms. In this image, I accented her with several shades of purple, a royal color to emphasize Her regal nature. She sits peacefully in meditation, for she has mastered all fear.

She holds Her center right hand out in the **mudra of giving**, for a leader must be willing to give as well as receive. In Her other right hand she holds a mala of amethyst, Her **connection to the cycle of life and liberation**.

In Her center left hand she holds a water vase, a symbol of **sacrifice and fulfillment**, and in Her other left hand she holds a scepter or staff, a symbol of Her **supernatural dominance**. Her heart chakra is open, for she is willing to be vulnerable. She holds no weapons, for Her victory is not through domination.

This Tara is sometimes described as atop a golden mountain, which is reflected in the background. Yet in this image, I have situated her in the valley between two mountains, for she is victorious over the peaks, but also over the valleys of our lives. The valley also forms a natural "V," Her symbol of victory. Tara is a natural leader, willing to accept responsibility for the benefit of all, and this requires stability in the midst of change.

I accented her number by a four-armed cross, a stable and balanced symbol. She is a source of stability.

The lithomancy stone for this Tara is **goldstone**, a very shiny rock, indeed.

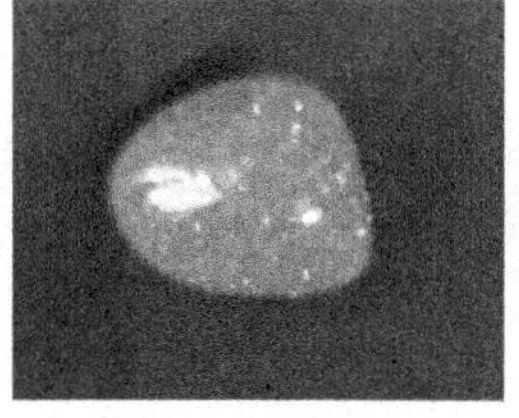

You have all that is needed to claim victory over the struggles you have faced, the peaks and also the valleys. Invite All Victorious Tara to help you find a stable place from which you can move forward. You have transcended obstacles, but you have other obstacles to face. Let your past guide you into your future.

PREMA'S COMMENTARY:

The garden is ready. Who enters the garden? Tara number 4, the victorious one. The one that has conquered anything that might inhibit Her full expression of enlightened mind, of mastery.

We imagine this Tara, the great victor, as a queen who has accomplished great things, entering into Her queendom. As she rides through the streets on Her royal elephant, the people are leaning out of the windows, throwing flowers upon Her and celebrating Her victory.

Even the celestial ones are celebrating Her victory, the great Buddhas and bodhisattvas, the ones who have mastered the Perfections, who are themselves the essence of the virtue. They are celebrating this victory.

The reflection into the Tarot: the Emperor. Four is a number that indicates a stable foundation. The earth is fertile. Now we are going to build the edifice in which our enlightened mind dwells.

We are going to build a civilization upon this verdant earth based on right relationship. We have a profound understanding of natural law.

We understand that everything changes profoundly, arising and passing away 360 times a second. We are victorious, because we have a complete understanding of the relationship of the sublime and the material.

#5: Sublime Intelligence

Tarot Archetype:
Hierophant
(Religion, group identification,
conformity, tradition, beliefs)

Tara #5 Praise:

Praise Her Whose Mantric Sound of
Tutare Hung
Fills the Realms of Desire,
All Directions All Space
She Tramples the Seven Worlds
with Her Feet
She has the Power
to Control and Summon them All

Tara of **Sublime Intelligence** gives the consistent wisdom that arises in the mind. She corresponds to the traditional tarot archetype of the hierophant, who reveals the sacred mysteries.

Tara is the rising sun, revealing all mysteries and illusions with Her brilliant light. She is a bright yellow and red, the reflection of the morning sky.

Her eyes are very important as she sees through all illusions. The light of the morning sun has broken the darkness of night and given you the opportunity to see clearly.

Tara #5 has two arms. Her right hand shows the protecting mudra, for she **protects against all ignorance**. Her left hand shows the mudra of the triple gem and holds the stem of a lotus, for our wisdom connects to our **three sources of refuge**, and this wisdom allows the **blossoming of highest mind**.

The sun rises behind Her, radiating a brilliant red throughout a limitless sky. The relationship to the hierophant also suggests an ordered mind, a disciplined mind, which allows for the freedom of mind expansion.

The number is 5, accented by a compass, for she fills all directions and all space. Through Tara of Sublime Intelligence, we can find true direction.

Tara #5 gives you discriminating awareness and the ability to see things clearly. While all may have been dark, the sun has risen. This golden Tara, auspicious in Her abundance, is also red, magnetizing and drawing others to you.

The lithomancy stone for this Tara is **citrine**, a translucent yellow stone good for health and wealth.

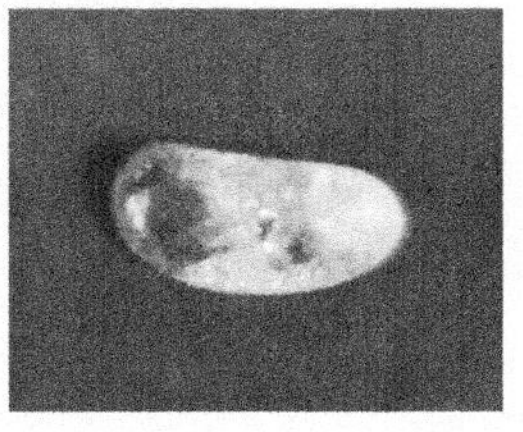

You have the great opportunity to share your insights and awareness with others. Your intelligence transcends book knowledge or even practical experience. You can transform multiple types of intelligence into awareness and action. Sublime indeed.

PREMA'S COMMENTARY:

This brings us to number 5, once known as the number of protection. We have laid the foundation, now we must build the structure according to hierarchical relationships.

We understand what is most important and what we are building upon. How are we bringing structure together? It is all the different aspects of our practices that lead us into fulfillment.

This is the analytical mind, the intelligence. We remind ourselves: we are here to manifest enlightened mind. That is the "I Will," the purpose of us being upon this earth.

We have the incredible treasure of this human opportunity where there are an equal amount of blessings and challenges. Here, in this great fertile environment, we are able to manifest the full blossoming of consciousness.

But we must have our structure in order. We must recognize why we are here, then we must also invoke our sources of refuge, so we know we can be continually brought back to our center should we lose our way.

This is the structure of intelligence, reflecting into the Tarot, number 5, the Hierophant.

We are looking at the Priest, the Pope, the one who heads the church, the one who declares to us that there is a hierarchy of consciousness, a hierarchy of practice. And so we align ourselves in an appropriate way.

#6: Worthy of Honor

Tarot Archetype:
The Lovers
(Love, union, relationships, values alignment, choices)

Tara #6 Praise:

Praise Her Whom Indra,
Agni, Vayu and Brahma
All the Worldly Gods Make Offerings to Her
Demons, Depraved Ones and
All Harmful Spirits
Bow in Deep and Complete
Surrender to Her

Tara is honored and respected for Her very nature, and so she is called **Worthy of Honor.**

She is a deep red, the color of magnetism, and she wears black, for she can be intensely ferocious if crossed. Yet she sits in a meditative pose. She draws others to Her, and even harmful spirits bow down to Her worth.

She has four arms. In Her center right hand, she holds a sword, which **cuts through all ignorance and confusion**. She holds a dorje (**lightning and power**) with Her other right hand.

With Her left hands she holds a rope (**liberation**) and displays the **threatening mudra**. She is sometimes known as the "Terrifier," for she demands respect of Gods and Demons.

Yet, she corresponds to the traditional Tarot archetype of the Lovers, which represents unity and balance. The primal forces of power and magnetism must surrender to wisdom and compassion in order to create this balance.

This also represents the balance between intrinsic and manifested deity. We honor Tara as an external force, the Bodhisattva, who achieved enlightenment. But the teachings emphasize that we have these qualities within ourselves and should use the external meditation like a magnet to draw out the inner qualities. The Tara within is also **Worthy of Honor**.

Two interlocking triangles create a six-pointed star to represent balance on the card. This shows the unity of projective and receptive principles. In the background, a full, red rose blossoms. Tara is the center of the rose, the unity holding the petals together. Like the delicate unfolding petals of a rose, this precious mortal life is temporary, but so worthwhile. The rose is also an offering to Tara, a sweet-smelling sacrifice to the one who merits all respect.

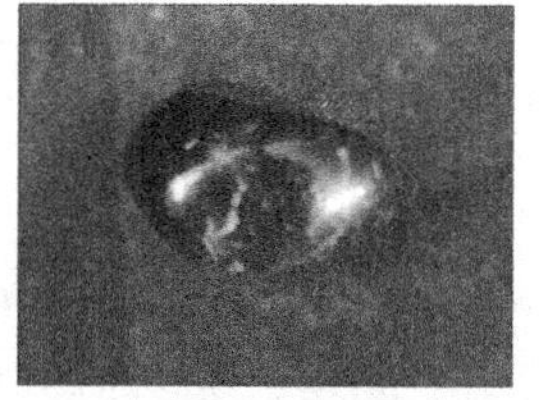

Her lithomancy stone is a **deep red garnet,** so dark it is nearly black.

Tara #6, **Worthy of Honor**, will remind you of your own inherent worth and dignity, along with that of all interconnected beings. Remember your worth. Remember who you are. Remind others that they, too, are worthy of honor.

PREMA'S COMMENTARY:

Tara number 6, She who is **Worthy of Honor**. This specific gesture of Tara was developed because of the circumstance of the imbalance that is within our current world system. Even in the world system from which Tara comes, there was this imbalance. We take note of it in the story of Her origin, when she vowed to remain in the body of a woman until the end of time. She wished to demonstrate that the female form was as worthy as a male to manifest awakening.

The symbol of six is the upper pointed triangle, the masculine, and the downward pointed triangle, the feminine, united, creating what is known in our world as the star of David. This six-pointed triangle, representing the union of heaven and earth, of male and female, of all polar opposites, its essence is out of balance, and this is one of the things that the practice of Tara addresses.

This Tara is also known as the Terrifier. Not only is she **Worthy of Honor**, but she commands honor and respect. Through millennia, the feminine has not been given its place. If it is not in equal balance with the masculine, then our great system of reflection is out of balance. This must be addressed.

We all must become aware of this, but women must declare for themselves that they are **Worthy of Honor**. They must reveal this within themselves.

This Tara calls this forth from us. This is not honoring women instead of men, but honoring the feminine within each man and woman. The feminine of the psyche must be recognized. The analytical power and the intuitive power have equal importance.

In this praise, all of the gods are acknowledging that she is **Worthy of Honor**, and they make offerings to Her, acknowledging that she too is a Buddha. And all demonic forces acknowledge Her enlightened accomplishment. We see the celestial beings, and we see the terrestrial beings uniting in their recognition of the divine feminine.

This reflects into the Lover card. Here we see a young man deciding to go with a young woman or with an older woman, following his lust or his inspiration.

This is a question that we must all face. In order to be **Worthy of Honor**, we must pursue the highest and most lofty goals. This is inherent in our consciousness.

We may travel the path of materiality, but we will soon be frustrated, until we turn toward the wisdom, until we turn toward the spirit. The reflected universal response of this turning is to bow in deep respect and honor.

#7: Invincible Courage

Tarot Archetype:
The Chariot
(control, will power, victory,
assertion, determination)

Tara #7 Praise:

Praise Her the One
Who Chants Tre and Pe
Defeating the Snares
and Schemes of enemies
With Right Leg Folded,
and Left Leg Outstretched
Shining in Splendor
Midst a Fierce Blazing Fire

Tara of **Invincible Courage** defeats all fears and dangers. She is unafraid of obstacles and dispels all confusion.

She is strong, powerful, and muscular. She has no fear in Her face, a willingness to meet all obstacles.

The background is a path, leading into oblivion, with a limitless sky filled with feathery clouds. This Tara corresponds with the traditional Tarot archetype of the Chariot, which is often about confusion and trials on the journey and the willingness to make tough choices in order to stay on the right path.

She threatens any who would challenge Her. She is turquoise blue, the color of communication and courage, and black, the color of wrath. She wears the skin of a tiger, fierce and untamed.

Tara #7 has four arms. Her right hands hold a sword (**dispelling ignorance**) and a wheel (**truth**), and Her left hands hold a rope (**liberation**) and show the **threatening mudra**.

Instead of a moon behind Her head, she is surrounded by flames, the fire of Her own wisdom and knowledge. She can face any challenge, for She is armed with truth and wisdom. In the background, the sky is limitless, but the end of the path is obscured. Sometimes we must face unknown challenges and obstacles on our path to liberation. We must hold on to courage in the face of all danger.

Tara #7 clearly and confidently moves forward. You are on a journey, and you cannot see your destination. You will find your way one step at a time. Acting out of courage is about facing your fears, and you have the power to do this. Powerful blue Tara dances into the future. She gives you the courage to speak your mind and face hostilities. You know the path, and you will overcome whatever obstacles you face.

The lithomancy stone for Tara #7 is **amazonite**, a turquoise blue in color. This stone reminds me of the amazon warrior women, great in courage.

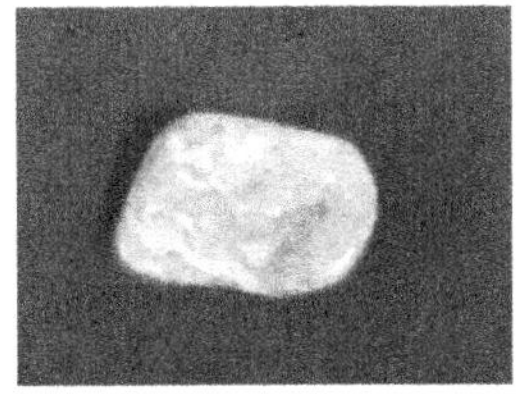

PREMA'S COMMENTARY:

Tara number 7: **Invincible Courage.** As we travel our journey of manifesting enlightened mind, there's every kind of circumstance that seems to stand in our way. Externally, we call these the snares and schemes of enemies, and of course, it takes great courage to face every challenge in life.

We are very fortunate to have Tara to call upon to assist us as we face these challenges. Even more important is to understand that these snares and schemes are within us, that we undermine ourselves. We have this sense of inadequacy that we have developed through our life that continually tells us we cannot do this, that we are not worthy. We must face this insidious murmuring or muttering in the background with great courage.

Number 7 in the Tarot is the **Chariot**. The Chariot is shown to be an individual with two horses, white and black, positive and negative aspects of mind. And the control? No reins! We must control these horses with the power of our mind.

#8: Destroys Negativity

Tarot Archetype:
Strength
(Strength, courage, patience, control, compassion)

Tara #8 Praise:

Praise Her, Ture,
Terrifying and Fierce
Conquering the Demon
who Obstructs
the Path of Dharma
Lotus Face Frowning
She Slays All Enemies of Truth
Harmful Emotions
and Veils of the Mind

Tara **Destroys Negative Thoughts and Emotions** that threaten our minds. She is a "destroyer" which is usually a "wrathful" trait, but rather than red or blue (the traditional wrathful colors), she is gold, the color of abundance. The best way to destroy negative thoughts and emotions is through positive thoughts and emotions.

She sits atop a makara, or sea monster. This represents the primordial depths of emotion, which are difficult to control. The makara unleashed may cause limitless pain and emotional turmoil, but as Tara controls the makara, it becomes a guardian. Our emotions can be great tools to help us find our way.

Tara #8 has four arms. In Her center right hand, she holds a branch of the Ashoka tree, which is sometimes called the **healer of sorrows**. It is said that Buddha was born beneath this tree, and it can heal suffering, especially that of women. With Her other right hand she holds a **wish-fulfilling jewel**. In Her left hands, she holds a vase (**fulfillment**) and a lotus (**blossoming of wisdom and purity**). Her supporting color is a deep pink, a combination of magnetic red and peaceful white.

Tara #8 corresponds to the tarot archetype of Strength, which emphasizes empowerment and trust. Negative thoughts and emotions erode our strength, particularly in relationships with other people. Only through destroying this negativity can we find our way through the illusions of separation from others, recognizing our interconnectedness.

In the background, Tara rises above clouds of gold. Tara rises above a golden fog, able to see clearly through the harmful emotions and veils of the mind. It is like the "golden hour" for art and photography—the moment just before twilight when light hits at an angle to illuminate the face with a golden glow.

Her number, 8, represents the possibility of infinite mind, and is accented by an interconnected, representing the cycle of emotions but also a chain of strength. Through mindfulness, we can defeat negative thoughts and emotions and find freedom. Gratitude for your abundance will give you greater perspective on the negative thoughts that bring you suffering. Number 7 in the Tarot is the Chariot. The Chariot is an individual with two horses, white and black, positive and negative aspects of mind. And the control? No reins! We must control these horses with the power of our mind.

The lithomancy stone for this Tara is **aragonite,** a richly colored deep opaque yellow, sometimes orange.

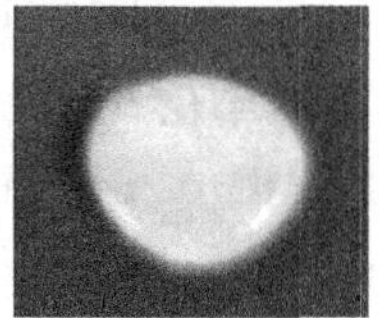

PREMA'S COMMENTARY:

This Tara, although she is golden in color, is ferocious. She is seen to be almost snarling, like a lioness. In fact, she reminds me of Simhamukha, the lion-faced Dakini, for she is powerful in that way. But this power is to assist us in destroying our tendencies toward negativity.

The mind is like water, seeking the lowest level. In that way mind goes to where we are most preoccupied with our difficulties and ruminates upon these problems, thinking negatively about others and about ourselves. This tendency must be dealt with very firmly and emphatically. It cannot be indulged in because it saps our strength and energy.

This reflects into the card **Strength**. What is our strongest point? Our strongest point is actually the weakest link, for that is where the connection breaks. That is where we must place our attention. Not at the strongest link, because of course that's going to carry through, but where is the weak point? Once we address the weak point, in fact, it becomes our strength because we have learned much information about how to make the weak point strong. It is necessary for us, with great power, to resist the tendency to negativity.

#9: True Refuge

Tarot Archetype:
The Hermit
(Soul-searching, introspection, being alone, inner guidance)

Tara #9 Praise:

Praise Her Whose Mudra
Is the Triple Gem
Her Fingers Perfectly
Adorning Her Heart
Centered in Her Hand
Radiating in All Directions
A Wheel of Shining,
Swirling, Spiraling, Brilliant Light

Tara of **True Refuge** represents the quiet, interior place to which we retreat, and she is also our connection to all of our sources of refuge, the Enlightened Ones, the teachings of the dharma, and our spiritual community.

She is related to the Hermit archetype, the introspective, quiet strength that holds wisdom deep within.

True Refuge is sometimes called the Saviouress of the Scented Sandalwood Forest, and so in this image she is found at the heart of a deep forest grove. She is green, the color of life and regeneration, accented with purple, the color of nobility and highest spirit.

She has four arms. She holds Her central hands above Her head in the mudra of **great joy**, holding a bell (**wisdom and impermanence**) and dorje (**lightning and power**). She holds Her other right hand in the **mudra of**

Refuge, indicating "Fear not, for I am a true source of Refuge."

Her other left hand holds the branch of the Ashoka tree, **healer of sorrows**. This Tara is mature, all-knowing, comforting, motherly, and beautiful. True Refuge nurtures and heals.

Her number, 9, resembles a spiral, accented by a radiant star with nine rays, representing the light she emanates throughout the universe. Tara of True Refuge gives a quiet place of reflection and grace to all who seek Her, but She is only found within.

The ritual of "taking refuge" in Buddhism is a commitment to the path of dharma. By making this commitment, a seeker looks to sources of refuge that will last.

Instead of seeking stability in the impermanence of objects or people or circumstances in samsara, the commitment to refuge encourages us to seek stability through three jewels.

Think about those who have inspired your path. Who are your teachers, for they have introduced you to the three jewels? The enlightened ones who inspire you? The teachings that bring you wisdom? The community or sangha which supports you?

These are your own sources of refuge. Take comfort in knowing that you are not alone and yet listen to the still, small voice within. Tara #9 will guide you.

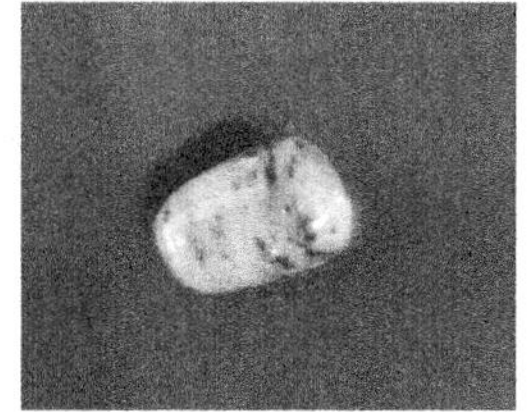

The lithomancy stone for Tara of True Refuge is **zoisite**, a fresh green stone, green like a deep forest.

PREMA'S COMMENTARY:

Tara number 9, **Lady of the Sandalwood Forest**, She who gives refuge. It is said that when Tara first appeared through the tears of the Lord of Compassion, she immediately went down to the south of India and took up residence in a sandalwood forest. There, she taught the animals.

She was first seen by a hunter who was moving through the forest. He noticed a light in the distance, and when he approached, he realized it was this radiantly beautiful woman, dressed in leaves, and at Her feet all the animals sat. The most violent animals with the most passive were sitting together, none being threatened by the other.

And when Tara saw him, she gave Her first teaching to a human being. The teaching was that of **refuge**, for she declared to him she would be a true source of refuge and explained what that meant.

The refuge that we seek is to come out of the confusion of our own mind, this misunderstanding of separation and isolation, to come into the warmth of unity, the understanding of interconnectedness.

Therein we find the **true refuge**. And those who give refuge are the ones who remind us of this, who remind us we are not only a part, we are also the whole, wondrous, brilliant mind of enlightenment.

Tara number 9, holding out Her hand, radiating light in all directions, inspiring us with Her brilliance.

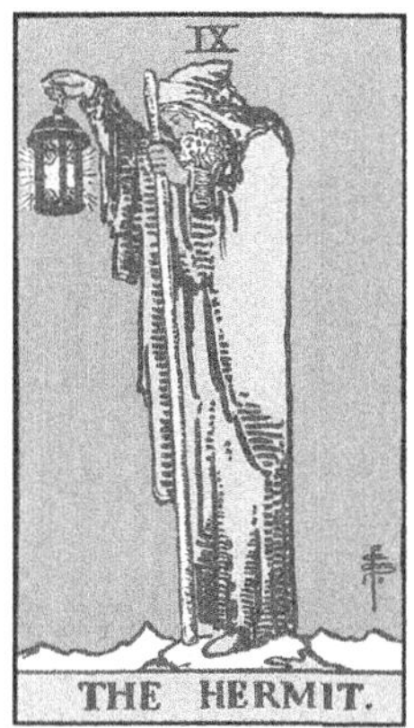

This reflects into the card of Tarot number 9, **The Hermit**, wisdom in the wilderness. In the forest we see the image of an elder, who is holding up the light.

This sense of wisdom being our true protection. We must turn towards that. **The Hermit** also represents the need to isolate, to go within, and to shut off the busyness of the world and all our myriad connections. We seek the source within.

#10: Joy & Laughter

Tarot Archetype:
Wheel of Fortune
(Good luck, karma, life cycles,
destiny, a turning point)

Tara #10 Praise:

Praise Her the One
Who Radiates Supreme Joy
Her Jeweled Diadem Ablaze
Shines a Garland of Light
She Bursts Out Laughing,
Exclaiming Tutare
Her Joyous Laugh
Brings the Worlds
Under Her Sway

Tara of **Joy and Laughter** sees the inconsistencies in life and finds humor in them. Like a child, she finds joy in all circumstances, recognizing the impermanence of all things.

Tara #10 is a red Tara of magnetism and power. Her laughter is contagious, filling all circumstances with light. After all, as Prema often says, it is "en-light-enment," not "en-heavy-ment" we seek.

Tara's laugh gives Her power over all the worlds because she has conquered all fear. Her garland of light reaches into places of greatest darkness.

She has four arms. She holds her center arms above Her head in a **mudra of joy**. Her other right hand holds a sword, which **cuts through ignorance**. Her other left hand holds a lotus, **rising above all obstacles**. She is seated but ready to move, with left leg pulled in and right leg moving forward.

She corresponds with the tarot archetype of the **Wheel of Fortune**, the constantly changing and spinning wheel of life. A wheel, the spinning reminder of potential and possibilities, accents her number, 10.

She teaches us to accept things as they come, even when they come with the force of a storm. Will things be destroyed? Perhaps. Even when the storm turns into a hurricane, a substantial force with the power to leave destruction in its wake, the best way to meet this uncertainty is through laughter.

The specific hurricane on this card is Hurricane Irene of 2014. This storm threatened the Hawaiian islands just before the annual Tara retreat I planned to attend. Fortunately, there was no damage to the camp, but it delayed us for several days and there were other obstacles. Prema encouraged to let go of our expectations and laugh about it.... and I sure had to let go of my expectations.

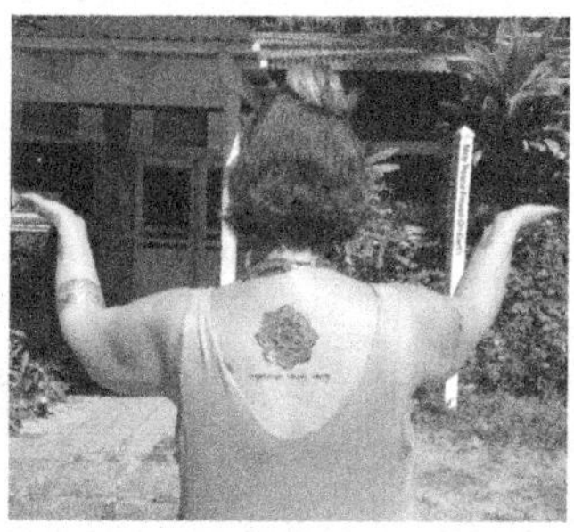

A temporary tattoo on my back on that trip

Because of circumstances outside of my control, I was losing my career. My marriage was falling apart. I was in recovery from cancer, but I still had some serious health challenges ahead. And a family member of mine died while I was on that trip... did I mention that Card #10 is my Birth Card? If I had been attached to that trip going exactly one way... well, it wasn't going to go that way. But the wheel turned. And turned again. And again. It keeps turning. I just try to keep up. In the meantime, I became good friends with **Lady Fortuna**, the Roman Goddess of Fortune who is also related to this card.

Laugh at the obstacles. Find ways to see your fears as ridiculous. This will bring you joy. Inevitably, red Tara of **Joy and Laughter** will help you get through some things you never thought you would face.

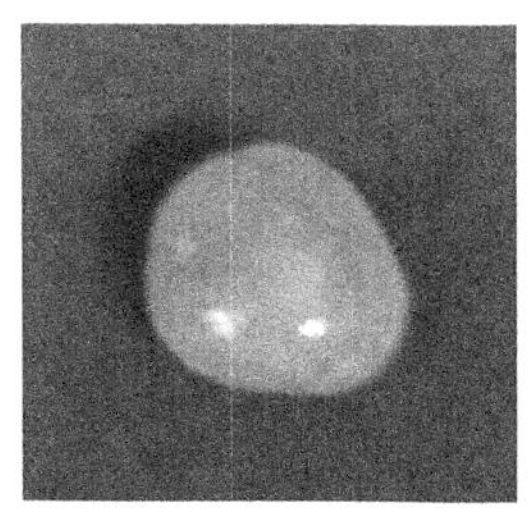

The lithomancy stone for Tara of Joy & Laughter is **carnelian**, a bright orange-red gem.

PREMA'S COMMENTARY:

Tara number 10, the Tara of **Joy and Laughter**. How essential it is to laugh as we journey this road of consciousness. Why is Tara laughing? Her laughter stems from our unfortunate habit of taking ourselves and the world so seriously. We continually become distracted by the various presentations of life. When we are on the wheel and the wheel is going up, things are looking good. We think they'll always be wonderful. We become very attached to this.

Of course, everything changes. When we are on the wheel and the wheel is going down, and we are having problems and difficulties, we tend towards depression. We take ourselves and the action that occurs to us so seriously. If we are able to see clearly the infinite possibilities of our mind and the dance of light and darkness in relation to its relativity, then we would laugh.

This reflects into the card, **The Wheel of Fortune**. We see the same great wheel, the wheel that goes up and down. The greatest wisdom is to say, no matter what occurs, this too shall pass. The laugh of the Goddess has been described in literature as the terrible laugh, because if one takes oneself seriously, then the last thing one is able to hear is this laugh. The laugh seems almost ruthless. But really it is loving and brilliant, calling us home to the truth.

#11: Distributor of Wealth

Tarot Archetype:
Justice
(Justice, fairness, truth, cause and effect, law)

Tara #11 Praise:

Praise Her who Commands
the Protectors of the Worlds
Through Her Inner Power
She Summons them All.
With Wrathful Frown
She Thunders the Syllable Hung.
Savior of the Poor,
She's the Giver of Wealth

Tara, **Distributor of Wealth,** is a wrathful equalizer. She gives all that is needed, and thus is the Savior of the poor, but she also takes away what is not needed, releasing our attachment and pride.

Tara #11 corresponds to **Justice**, which is sometimes also called **Karma**. Justice brings balance, harmony and equilibrium, just as karma returns that which has been sent out. This Tara is equally concerned with justice, giving benefit and wrath in turn. She is like a thundercloud, whose rain can heal the land but destroy some crops. She is a force beyond our personal desires, constantly working for the greater scheme of life. This Tara is dark blue, the color of a dark thundercloud, but Her garments are rich gold. She rains down wealth among those she chooses. She holds two hooks commonly used to prod elephants, thus symbolically **prodding our sluggish minds into action** and segregating us from doubt.

She is thin, ferocious, with wild hair flying, able to command forces of nature. In the background, dark thunderclouds gather, ready to unleash their force, but light also shines, balancing the darkness. She is older than many other Taras, showing Her wrathful Crone face. Strong, thin, but with a full belly, she commands immediate respect. She looks out at the world, sees the inequity, and like the Christ overturning the money changers' tables, she won't stand for it. She is all about balance. A set of scales, symbol of balance and justice, accents her number, 11. Tara will bring all things into balance according to Her greater scheme.

Think about your own boundaries. Are you acting in a fair and just manner? Is your life out of balance? When things are out of balance, danger is imminent. You cannot ignore the rest of the world—they need what you have to give — but you must balance your own needs before you can give fully to others.

Think about the world. The resources in our world are vastly out of balance. Tara #11 is our call to action. Find your own way, big or small, to change the world.

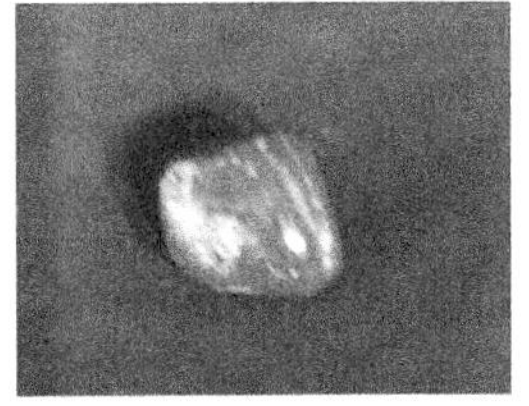

The lithomancy stone for this Tara is **lapis lazuli**. Its dark blue color has occasional inclusions of gold, and it has been prized in cultures dating back as far as ancient Egypt and Sumeria as a sacred stone.

PREMA'S COMMENTARY:

Tara number 11, **Distributer of Wealth**. This Tara reflects the different ways in which wealth is considered in Her practice. In the more ancient Suryagupta system, this Tara is blue-black like a thundercloud, representing wrath, because wealth is not appropriately distributed. In the later systems of practice, such as Atisha, this Tara is seen as gold, the Giver of Wealth. But the praise tells us very clearly, she starts by commanding in a wrathful, determined way. She is demanding that the protectors of the world fulfill their promise. The wealth has not been adequately distributed. And by commanding the protectors, she is stimulating them to provide for this redistribution. In that way, she addresses the poor and gives nourishment and whatever is needed to those who are not so blessed. The reflection of this into the Tarot is the card of **Justice**. It is not only our action that causes us to have karmic reflections of difficulty, but our thoughts.

Justice, the card of karma: what we do reflects back to us. This is a vast understanding that every thought reflects back, every action reflects back. Like a stone dropped into a lake, the ripples will go out until they touch every shore and then they will reflect back, multiplied. Every act, every thought, every word has consequence. And so it is the redistribution, not only of our wealth, but of our wisdom and our power.

#12: Auspicious Beauty

Tarot Archetype:
The Hanged Man
(Suspension, restriction, letting go, sacrifice)

Tara #12 Praise:

Praise Her Whose Diadem
is a Crescent Moon.
Her Ornaments Ablaze
Stream Shining Light.
The Buddha Amitabha
Sits Atop Her Hair.
He Radiates a
Stream of Dazzling Light.

Tara #12 is golden, the color of Auspicious Abundance. She is intensely beautiful, drawing others to Her with Her sensuality and gaze. In this image, she is adorned with golden orange scarves, representing the fertility of the second chakra, the womb and sensuality.

Tara of **Auspicious Beauty** represents the type of fertility needed to bring forth life. A woman's body is the only way humans can grow babies. This fertility is also the power of the land to bring forth new life every spring.

Yet, Tara of **Auspicious Beauty** also represents the sacrifice related to birth, for in any birthing process, there is pain and difficulty. A new mother sacrifices many of Her own needs for the needs of the child. The earth must also sacrifice Her fruits in the autumn in order to plant the seeds for the spring.

Tara #12 corresponds to the **Hanged Man** in the traditional tarot, who represents choices and sacrifices, though the choices and sacrifices are made in order to bring about future glory. The **Hanged Man** card often features a tree, so I chose a background of a radiant autumn tree for this card. The glorious autumn leaves also represent Tara's beauty, but also the cycle of death and rebirth in nature. In areas where winter brings freezing temperatures, deciduous trees must lose their leaves to preserve the life of the tree. The leaves die for the sake of the whole. Autumn is a time for sacrifice in order to bring about rebirth.

She has eight arms. In Her right hands she holds a dorje (**lightning and power**), a trident (**the three-fold refuge**), a hook (**stimulating the mind**), and a sword (**cutting through illusion**).

In Her left hands she holds a conch (**wish-fulfillment**), a hook (**stimulating the mind**), a scepter (**dominance**) and a vase (**fulfillment and sacrifice**).

A waxing crescent moon, the auspicious rising part of the lunar cycle, accents the number 12 for Tara of **Auspicious Beauty**. Twelve is a number of completion, as there are twelve hours in a day, twelve months in a year, twelve houses in the zodiac, etc.

Thus, Tara of **Auspicious Beauty** is the complete cycle, from birth to death.

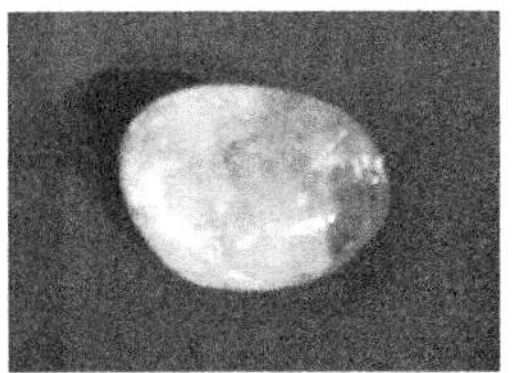

Her lithomancy stone is **honey quartz**.

PREMA'S COMMENTARY:

Tara number 12, **Auspicious Beauty**. Auspicious means that which brings forth life, sometimes translated as good fortune or good luck.

This Tara is seen as the most radiant woman, covered with gems and jewels. The crescent moon is in Her hair. All of this represents the feminine in its fruit, because fruit represents the great sacrifice. When fruit arises automatically, that fruit bursts apart. Seeds are spread, and new life arises. So at the moment of its greatest ripeness, that is its greatest sacrifice. It represents what bringing forth life actually means, living with abundance, with the greater whole in mind. This Tara has Amitabha at the top of Her hair, he the Buddha of infinite light. She arises from light; she radiates light, and she is the essence of light.

This Tara reflects into the card "**The Hanged Man**," a symbol of sacrifice, an image that comes from Scandinavia. In one of the ancient cultures there, they used to hang a man upside down, and when the blood rushed to his head, eventually he would have visions. It was a great sacrifice for him, but these visions enabled him to inform his community, to see deeply into that feminine wisdom, the pool of becoming. Tara number 12, the Tarot Hanged Man, reveals the auspiciousness of sacrifice, the beauty of life in its fruit.

#13: Irresistible Truth

Tarot Archetype:
Death
(Endings, beginnings, change,
transformation, transition)

Tara #13 Praise:

Praise Her Blazing
Like a Fire at the End of Time
Abiding in the Center
of a Garland of Flames.
Her Left Leg Folded,
Her Right Leg Outstretched
Giving Joy to the Prayerful,
All Obstacles are Subdued.

Red Tara of **Irresistible Truth** is the magnetic fire, constantly drawing us like moths to flame. We are drawn to the warmth, but fire consumes and destroys all that is not pure.

This Tara corresponds to the traditional Tarot archetype of **Death**, which represents change and transformation. Thus, through the fire we are transformed, the phoenix rising from the ashes.

She is surrounded by flames, the powerful emanation of Her wisdom. Her body is like a flame, sinewy, eyes magnetic. She is beautiful in Her ferocity, with an underlying sense of mystery and terror.

She is a deep, magnetic red with four arms. In Her right hands she holds a sword, which **cuts through illusions**, and an arrow, which represents **consciousness**. In Her left hands she holds a wheel, which represents **truth**, and a bow, which represents **direction**. She directs us to the raw truth of dharma and the recognition of illusion.

A volcanic eruption emphasizes the force and power of Her fiery presence, melting the very rock and destroying all in Her path. And yet, like the volcano cools to form new land, she creates through this destruction.

Her number, 13, is often viewed with superstition and fear, but it is also a number of great power. When you can tap into your fears, you can control them.

Tara provides the power we need to understand truth. Think about the truths you are avoiding. These are the things you know in the deep caverns of your mind, but you keep hiding them.

Tara #13 will not allow you to hide from them any more. What are you afraid to admit to yourself?

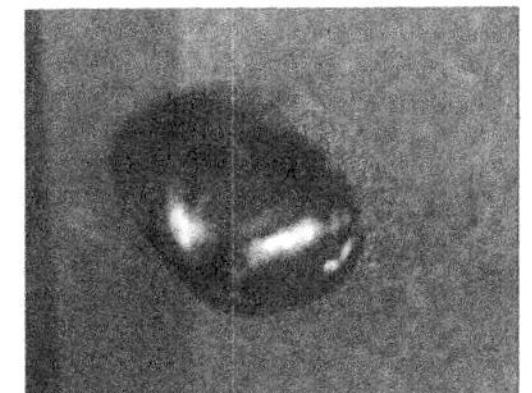

Her lithomancy stone is **black jet**, a powerful resin connecting to the ancient world.

PREMA'S COMMENTARY:

Tara number 13, **Irresistible Truth**. This Tara, brilliantly red, is seated in the midst of wisdom flames. The element of irresistibility means that she is charismatic and magnetic. She attracts others to Her, like a moth to the flame. She seeks to attract others so that she may bless them, inform them, teach them, and benefit them.

Magnetism is a very important part of this practice because it shows us that being able to attract others is not for our own self-aggrandizement or for ourselves to show how wonderful or famous we are. It is to enable us to be able to bless them and help them. Her stance is powerful, for she is making a powerful statement.

This reflects into the card **Death**, the ultimate transformation. At this point, we must realize that all form must be relinquished into the pool of transformation. This is an extremely powerful, compelling moment in our consciousness, when we must be willing to let go fully.

#14: Ferocious Compassion

Tarot Archetype:
The Devil
(Bondage, addiction, sexuality, materialism)

Tara #14 Praise:

Praise Her Who Strikes
the Earth with Her Palm
Earth's Foundation is Shaken
as She Tramples with Her Feet,
With A Wrathful Glance
and the Powerful Sound of Hung,
She Subdues Confusion,
Throughout the Seven Realms

Tara of **Ferocious Compassion** is like the mother who must punish Her child to keep that child from harm. When we pursue a path of self-destruction, this Tara forces us to change.

She corresponds to the traditional tarot archetype of **the Devil**, which often represents a warning. This Tara warns us not to become trapped in our self-destructive behaviors, and Her intervention is strong, sometimes painful. In Her original Tibetan form, she is a fierce black Tara. Within the Mandala practice, she is purple, a combination of red (magnetism) and blue (discipline).

Tara #14 has three faces, white to the right as the Maiden moon and red to the left as the Mother. The Crone is the center, as she is fate, the one who decides who should live and who should die.

In Her traditional Tibetan form, she has six arms. In Her right hands, she holds a sword (**to cut through**

illusions), a hook (**stimulating the mind**), and a scepter (**showing Her sovereignty**). In Her left hands she holds a skull-cup, from which she drinks **sacrificial blood**, a wheel (**truth**) and a rope (**liberation**). She is adorned with skulls and dances upon the corpse of an enemy, which represents **misunderstanding**. Her long necklace is a necklace of skull beads, reminding us of death.

This fierce visage at first may seem alarming, but it is with all compassion that she reminds us of the temporal nature of our very lives. Life is fragile and impermanent, and we must constantly remember genuine compassion.

The background of this card is the cracked earth, for she stamps Her hands and feet, shaking the foundations of all we know. Yet she is also the breath of compassion, symbolized by the wind, bringing us understanding and wisdom. Her number, 14, is significant, for this is our only departure from the traditional Tarot numbering. Tara of **Ferocious Compassion** corresponds to #15, the Devil. She shakes things up, never allowing one to settle into complacency and stagnation.

Her lithomancy stone is **sugilite**, an opaque purple stone with deep black inclusions.

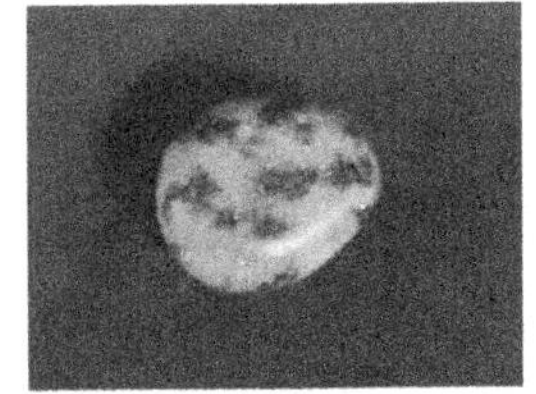

PREMA'S COMMENTARY:

Tara number 14 is the most wrathful Tara. She is black. We often dress Her in purple or in blue, the dark colors that represent that ability to penetrate.

This is the Tara that says "no!" She says it with great ferocity. The metaphor is as if she were a mother who sees Her child about to run in front of a car. She may shout in a loud and wrathful way in order to stop the child, but this is only done out of love. And so the ferociousness comes from a pool of compassion. We must be able to display ferocity as well as peace in our presentation.

It is at this place in the relationship between the cards in the Tarot that we must change the order of the cards. In the Rider-Waite deck, the Devil card is number 15. I believe this corresponds best to Tara #14, Ferocious Compassion because of the darkness of the two figures.

The Devil represents the inability to make the right choice. It requires a very firm stand to face up to the temptations -

to turn away from the truth, to turn away from the spirit, to turn away from integration, and to turn into fragmentation. We feel pulled apart by these choices that we have. We must take the most powerful stance against this dangerous condition.

#15: Serene Peace

Tarot Archetype:
Temperance
(Balance, moderation, patience, purpose, meaning)

Tara #15 Praise:

Praise Her the One
Who is Bliss, Virtue, and Peace
Her Activity is the Peace
Beyond Suffering
With the Pure Sounds
of Om and Soha
She Purifies
all Negativity and Guilt

Tara of **Serene Peace** brings together all the qualities of a quiet mind, allowing beauty and light to shine forth.

She corresponds to **Temperance**, the card that shows the alchemical process where all elements combine magically to form something new. Similarly, this Tara purifies negativity, combining many elements to bring about harmony.

She rests in front of an idyllic, clear ocean, and a dove, symbolic of peace, accents the number 15. This calm presence of mind is completely possible, offered by Tara once attachments and delusions are released.

She is radiant, white with six arms. In Her top right hand, She holds a mala (**the complete cycle of existence**). The mala is also a source of peaceful meditation practice. 108 beads in a continuous circle, these sacred objects are used for mantra and breath meditation. They are a tangible tool used to bring inner peace.

In Her other right hand, She holds the mudra of **perfect giving** and a scepter (representing Her **sovereignty**). Thus, She is above the mundane world, but She is willing to give Her peace and grace to others. This peace is available, even within the world of samsara.

In Her left hands she holds a lotus (**purity**), a vase (**fulfillment**) and a cup filled with fruits (**auspicious manifestation**). Her wealth is abundant, for She has created peaceful fulfillment out of the darkest of places. She is complete equanimity, accepting all things, having attained true inner peace.

Tara of **Serene Peace** is the maiden that follows the crone of Ferocious Compassion. If you look at the 22 Taras as a continuous story, often a dark or wrathful Tara is followed by a peaceful one. We go through these cycles continuously.

Another important practice of peace is finding it during times of frustration, when the world is not as idyllic as this illustrates. How do you calm the mind when it whirls and swirls with the storms? So many spiritual practices begin with finding a "happy place," a place of peace, calm, and comfort. Imagine this image as that place within.

The lithomancy stone for Serene Peace is **blue lace agate**, a light blue stone with gentle waves of color stripes, like the waves of the ocean.

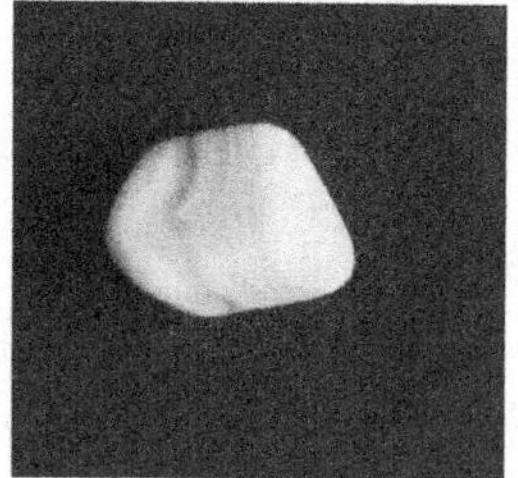

PREMA'S COMMENTARY:

Tara number 15, **Serene Peace.** We are now addressing the integration of all of life's experiences. It is a tendency in our world to feel that people are good or bad. If they make mistakes, then they are labeled bad. But in this system of practice, mistakes are simply that: mistakes. We cannot learn without making mistakes. The idea of feeling guilty for making a mistake does not fit into this scheme of practice. We can't hide it or pretend that it didn't happen. We must acknowledge that we were heading in a wrong direction perhaps, but we also should not allow it to color our feeling of ourselves as inherently divine beings.

This Tara calls us to integrate all of our past experiences and the great practice of purification. We recognize and regret when we have made a mistake. We renew our commitment to manifesting enlightened mind and remind ourselves that we have sources of refuge to support us. Then we remedy the circumstances. We resolve not to make the mistake again if we can help it. In this way, we purify the activity.

The reflection into the Tarot is Temperance. We see this understanding of integration. We see an angelic being, white just like Tara number 15, calling us to integrate all the different aspects of ourselves in order to manifest the fullness of our aspirations.

#16: Destroyer of Attachment

Tarot Archetype:
Tower
(Disaster, upheaval,
sudden change, revelation)

Tara #16 Praise:

Praise Her Rejoicing in
the Turning Wheel of Dharma
She Completely Destroys
All Enemies of Truth
Her Ten Mantric Syllables
Circle Within Her Heart
She Arises in Our Pure Awareness
with the Syllable Hung

Tara **Destroys Attachments,** those things we hold on to so tightly, our joys, our wealth, our senses, our conditioned existence. These things do not belong to us. No matter how much we want the "good" things in life to stay the same, the inevitable truth is that all things change. Through our attachment, we suffer when we lose that we would prefer to keep.

After the peaceful calm of #15, this Tara brings on the storm in truly terrifying ferocity. Yet she holds equanimity, seated in meditation. She holds a deep calm and fearlessness. She does what must be done, calmly and without hesitation.

Corresponding to the archetype of the Tower, which is about change and release from bondage. We are shackled to our attachments, and Tara destroys those shackles. In the background rises a fierce tornado, a natural tower which destroys all things in its wake. The tornado necessarily brings destruction and change. It is a force unto itself.

Tara, Destroyer of Attachment, is the color of red coral, a stone sacred in Tibetan and other cultures. She is wearing turquoise blue and accented by amber, two other sacred stones. She is the very epitome of the wealth and preciousness we are asked to release.

She holds a trident in Her right hand, reminder of the **three sources of Refuge**, and a branch of the Ashoka tree in Her left hand, the **sorrowless tree**. If we release our grasping and clinging, then we can truly be free from sorrow. Our sources of Refuge help us on this path.

She is mature, beautiful, and capable... a bit of a revolutionary. She is powerful, but joyful. She rejoices in the release, for the very act of destroying attachments brings freedom from suffering.

This Tara will bring about change, the turning of the wheel. Do what needs to be done, but then relax into the change. It cannot harm you.

The lithomancy stone for this Tara is **red coral**, a stone that was once a living thing but is now something else entirely.

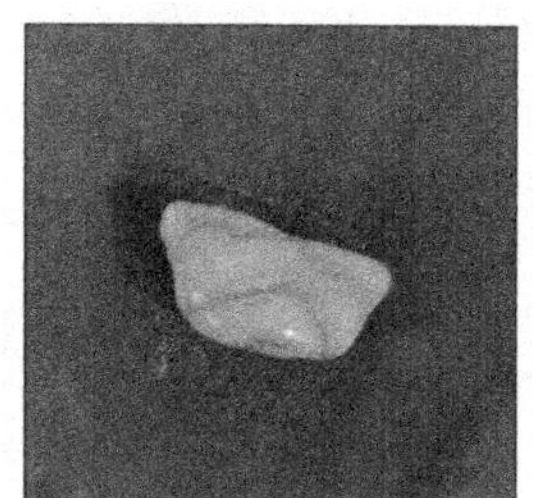

PREMA'S COMMENTARY:

Tara number 16: The Destroyer of Attachment. Arising from the purity of our own mind, the power of the mantra holds us stable. When the circumstances of life knock us off our center, we expect the world and its vast array of diversity to satisfy us. Then we are going to find ourselves unstable. In this way, we must at every moment be ready to let go of whatever it is that we cling to.

We must remain open and free. This does not mean that we ignore our responsibilities and our efforts or even a continuity of pleasure. It means that we do not cling to anything expecting it to provide us with stability, clarity, or satisfaction. We must destroy the tendency to attachment.

The Tarot card that is reflected by this powerful Tara is **the Tower**, a great symbol of unattachment. We see what appears to be a solid edifice, a stone tower.

But lightning coming from the sky causes the tower to tip and the individuals who have taken refuge there are falling out, the great moment of unattachment. The lightning from the sky represents heaven impregnating earth with inspiration, transformation, and the great letting go. New birth cannot arise unless we let go of old forms.

#17: Bliss & Joy

Tarot Archetype:
The Star
(Hope, spirituality, renewal,
inspiration, serenity)

Tara #17 Praise:

Praise Her Ture the Swift One
Arising from the Seed Word Hung
She Stamps Her Feet Shaking
the Greatest Mountain Peaks.
Mount Kailash,
Mount Mandara and Meru,
The Three Worlds Tremble
Beneath Her Dancing Feet

Tara of **Bliss & Joy** dances in the knowledge that she has conquered all confusion and doubt. Once we release all attachments, we are free to soar on wings of light.

She corresponds to the Tarot archetype of **the Star**, which represents confidence and intuition. A star accents her number. She is the clarity and light which guides us to true understanding.

She is a salmon color wearing yellow, colors of a sunset. These colors represent the magnetism of fire and the gold of abundance, both tempered by the white of merit, long life, and peace.

She raises Her two center arms above Her head in the **mudra of joy,** holding hooks that stimulate the mind. These hooks remind me of the scythe that is often associated with death, but in this context, they represent the freedom that death can imply.

She holds Her other right hand in the mudra of giving, open to the world. She gives bliss to all who need it. Her other left hand holds a lotus, the purification and blossoming of **highest mind**, upon which rests a sacred text. The text represents the **dharma**, or truth, as it is revealed to us through the teachings.

She sits upon a swan with spread wings, symbol of **freedom and liberation**. In the background is a generous burst of golden fireworks. The moment of blissful ecstasy is like this burst, temporary but joyful, beautiful, but somewhat dangerous. She reminds us again that bliss and joy come through the release of attachments.

She is pure ecstasy, young, beautiful, and free. This state of bliss eradicates suffering, even if only for a moment. Take pleasure in the euphoria. Though you know it will not last forever, it is true in the moment.

The lithomancy stone for this Tara is **rose quartz**, a stone often associated with self-love. The bliss and necessity of self-love is a triumph indeed.

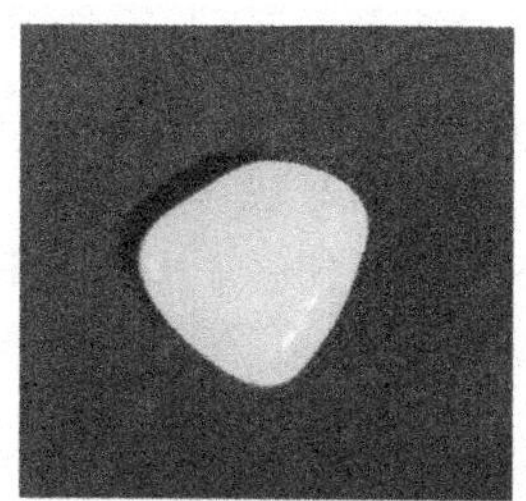

PREMA'S COMMENTARY:

This leads us to Tara number 17: the Tara of Bliss and Joy. When we have truly let go, this is the realm that we enter.

Tara means "star." One of the translations of Her name is literally "that which is radiant with light." In Her praise she dances upon the most solid parts of our planet, the great mountain peaks. Everything is shaking underneath Her blissful feet for she has declared the great impermanence and the joy and bliss that arises from truly letting go and understanding deeply the essence of unattachment.

This Tara reflects into the Star card of the tarot. It represents the fulfillment of practice, the experience of bliss when one releases attachment. Attachment restricts the natural flow of energy, preventing us from experiencing our natural emotional state – bliss.

We see a beautiful woman in the card, naked, free from anything that might hold Her back. She is completely unattached to conventional obligations of society. This allows Her to freely offer the nectar of Her intuition. She is one with the natural order. Like the kundalini energy rising up the spine, there is an explosion of great joy.

#18: Transformer of Poison

Tarot Archetype:
The Moon
(Illusion, fear, anxiety,
insecurity, subconscious)

Tara #18 Praise:

Praise Her Who Holds
the Moon in Her Hand
A Heavenly Ocean
Reflecting the Peaceful Deer
She Chants the Syllables of
Tare Tare Pe
With this Blessing
all Poisons are Transformed

Tara, **Transformer of Poisons,** takes our confusions, our difficulties and our challenges and transforms them into blessings and understanding. She represents intuition, reflection, suffering, and transformation.

A white Tara, she represents long life, good fortune, merit, wisdom, and good health. Whatever the poisons are, be they poison of the mind or body, she has the power to transform. Her secondary colors, blue and purple, show Her ferocity and unwillingness to back down in the face of danger. She will take what is given and transform it into something beautiful, even if the process is full of pain.

The Transformer of Poisons is usually associated with the peacock. Legend says this bird would eat poisons, but instead of dying, he would transform them into the beautiful plumage of the tail. The peacock is a male bird who uses these feathers to attract a female. The beauty of our transformation can be used to attract others to us to bring them benefit.

Her two hands hold a moon disc, an image of **intuition and reflection**. The moon holds power over the cycles of our oceans and our bodies, yet its power is mysterious. Often the moon is associated with intuition and female power, along with the deeper subconscious. Tara holds onto intuition as a tool, and she fluctuates as our own lives cycle through this varied existence.

Her head is tilted slightly to the left, for we have **mastered the power of aversion**. She faces that which is difficult. Her crown is intricately adorned, for she relies on the **highest level of mind**. She sits in seated meditation, focusing on the internal transformation.

She corresponds to the traditional Tarot archetype of the Moon, which often represents unseen enemies and the need for clarity. This is similar to the poisons of our minds, which creep into our consciousness like hidden enemies, sabotaging our good intentions.

She is beautiful, peaceful, mature, and capable. Seated in calm meditation, holding the moon that reflects our deepest mind, Tara transforms all poisons.

Her lithomancy stone, **peacock ore**, reflects all of the brilliant colors of a peacock.

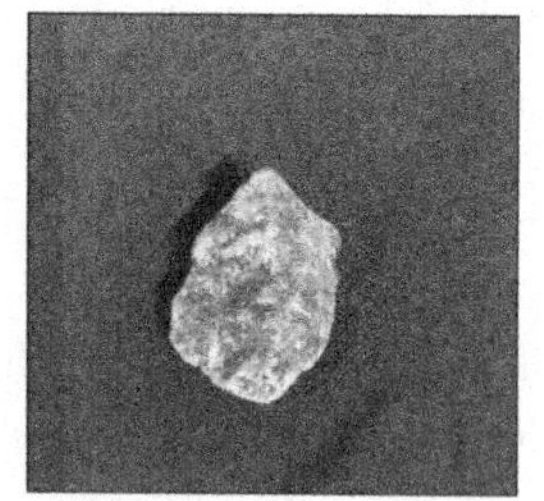

PREMA'S COMMENTARY:

Brilliantly white, holding the moon in Her hands, Tara #18,

Transformer of Poison, is the perfect metaphor reflecting into the Moon card. This is the moment in consciousness when we realize that we are able to see clearly into the depths of our mind's essence. We notice that within that depth there are the subtle poisons that are driving us into positions of instability. However, we have gained enough power, enough presence, to take this poison and consume it, to integrate it fully so that it becomes, like the peacock who also eats poison, the radiance of our display, the radiance of our beautiful peacock feathers.

What is it that we are displaying? The highest expression of the poison we integrated. As we come to terms with these deep underlying aspects of our own mind, we learn how to guide others who are so afflicted. The greatest challenge becomes our work, our ministry, our expression of enlightened mind, our blessing to the world.

The Moon card is often seen as a frightening thing, because when are faced with these subtle aspects of mind, it seems that all we have gathered together, all the wonder, all the beauty, all the awareness, all the transcendence, is about to be destroyed. We must remain firm. We must not be frightened of these poisons. We must learn like the peacock to consume them and to allow it to display our radiance.

#19: Remover of Sorrows

Tarot Archetype:
The Sun
(Fun, warmth, success, positivity, vitality)

Tara # 19 Praise:

Praise Her the One on Whom
the Celestial Rulers Rely
The Shining Ones and Spirits
Make Offerings to Her
Joyously Protecting
She is Radiant with Light
Dispelling Quarrels and Nightmares,
She Ends All War

Tara **Removes all Sorrows** and afflictions, healing our negativities and pain. She rids the world of negativity and sorrow and defeats nightmares and war.

She corresponds to **the Sun** of the tarot, which is the radiance, optimism and self-understanding. She is the partner of the Moon, the Transformer of Poisons. The two cards are mirrors to each other.

Both are white, representing long life, good fortune, merit, wisdom, and good health. Both are seated, but while Transformer of Poisons has Her legs pulled in, this Tara sits with one leg extended, quick to reach out to others.

Instead of a round moon, in Her two hands she holds a triangle, which represents the **power of fire** to burn away suffering. The moon is often considered a feminine symbol, while the upward pointing triangle is masculine. Its power is projective rather than receptive. Instead of tilting Her head to the left, she tilts to the right, **mastering the power of desire**, though she wears the intricate crown to represent **highest mind.** Instead of cool colors accenting Her peaceful white form, she wears the warm colors of burgundy and gold, magnetism and abundance.

She is radiant, beautiful, and mature. She has seen pain and suffering, but she holds the power to peace and transformation. But unlike the Moon, which calls upon the wisdom within for this transformation, the Sun radiates the light of wisdom outward, bringing that illumination to others.

Burning away pain requires revealing the negativities, opening up to one's deepest, darkest secrets. When these negativities are revealed, our deep connection with others leads to the power of forgiveness. This transforms anger, hatred, and war.

In the image behind Her flows a waterfall, symbol of our deepest emotions, sorrows and pain. Like a waterfall, these emotions cannot be dampened or stopped, but must be allowed to flow. If we hold on too tightly, the water can destroy. But if we remove sorrows, the light of the sun shining through the water brings life and liveliness to the world.

The lithomancy stone for this Tara is a **clear quartz crystal**, clear like the melting snow or ice.

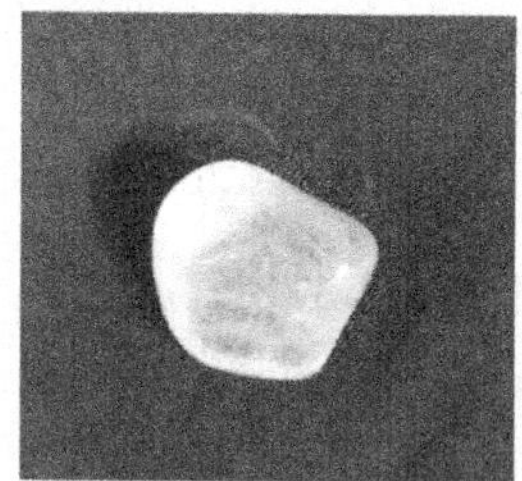

PREMA'S COMMENTARY:

Number 19, the **Remover of Sorrows.** This Tara is also radiantly white, but now she is making a statement. Her joy is going to transform the world. She has fully integrated all the aspects of Her nature. She sees that at the heart of our world's instability there is aggression, conflict, and war, leading to nightmares. Her way is to appear in the midst of conflict and with Her radiance eliminate the cause of conflict, the mind's instability. She removes the instability through the radiance of Her beauty and Her joy.

This is where we see the absolute nature of reality: conflict arises, but in the light of the sun it simply is no longer useful. There is nothing to fight against. There is open, brilliant space. When we become capable of experiencing and resting in the true nature of mind, there is only brilliance. There is no shadow. In one of Tara's stories, two armies have arrived on the battlefield. She appears between the armies, and she is so beautiful and brilliant that they forget why they came. The source of their aggression simply melts away in the presence of Her joyful light.

This Tara reflects into **the Sun** card, the radiance of beauty, joy and light. The child waves a banner of victory, just as Tara brought victory to both armies by eliminating their need to fight.

#20: Radiant Health

Tarot Archetype:
Judgment
(Judgement, rebirth, inner calling, absolution)

Tara #20 Praise:

Praise Her the One
Who is Radiant with Light
Her Clear Eyes Full Like
the Sun and the Moon
Chanting Hara Hara
and the Syllable Tutare
She Removes All Afflictions
and the Fiercest Illnesses

Tara of **Radiant Health** cures the illnesses of mind, body and spirit, for we are holistic beings. No part is whole without the others.

We are also connected to one another, all sentient beings, in a vast web of interconnectedness. This Tara radiates Her light into all parts of this web, healing all afflictions and illnesses in our communities.

She corresponds to the Tarot archetype of Judgment, which is about responding to messages, making decisions and connections to community. **Radiant Health** is more connected to community than ever as we are emerging from this worldwide pandemic.

When a part of the body is ill, it sends a message, often in the form of pain or discomfort, so that this illness can be attended. Similarly, an illness in the mind, spirit, or community will send messages in order to find healing. Too often in our modern society we treat pain with pain-killers rather than investigating the cause of the pain.

Tara encourages us to find the cause, to shine light on the holistic self, and to heal rather than hide our pain. She is copper in color, a rich combination of the deep red of magnetism and the deep gold of abundance. The metal copper is often said to have healing and restorative qualities.

She holds in Her two hands a vase containing **superb accomplishments** and the **realization of the nature of the mind**. The vase represents the elixir of life. Tara's elixir is not a physical medicine, but an understanding, a fulfillment of the mind's possibilities.

She sits in seated meditation, available to all who need Her but waiting until they are ready.

Tara's clear eyes shine like the sun and the moon. She is twilight, the moment while the sun is setting but the moon begins to rise. She is the threshold, the place between the worlds. She is the connection between all things.

An intricate knot accents her number, for we are all intricately connected to one another. In order to heal ourselves, we must heal the whole.

The lithomancy stone for Radiant Health is sunstone.

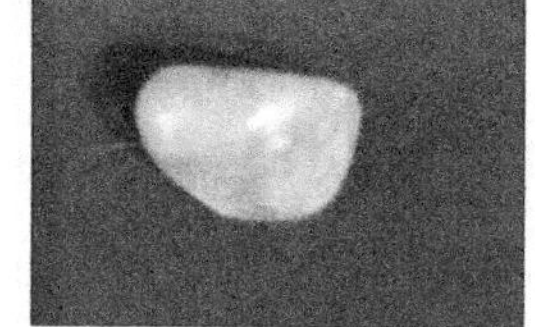

PREMA'S COMMENTARY:

Tara number 20 is often called the "mountain going mendicant." Copper-colored, she is often seen to be traveling through the most remote areas of the planet gathering herbs and minerals in order to make medicine. Her work is to deal with group Karma, that which produces the horrible epidemics that we all suffer from.

Guru Rinpoche spoke about this current time, saying that there would be great environmental destruction and warning us that this destruction would also bring about terrible diseases. He gave predictions for this time. One of them was that there would appear women who would move through the world bringing peace and inspiration, the healing necessary. These are manifestations of Tara. We feel this dance is a perfect expression of Guru Rinpoche's prediction, the perfect antidote to our sense of inadequacy and helplessness.

The reflection into the tarot is the Judgement card. We see this group karmic situation, as it arises again and again, as we are born again and again together in different formations, different cultures, each one dealing with whatever has been created in the past. Moving forward into the future, let us resolve now to move from a place of unity and interconnectedness.

#21: Complete Enlightenment

Tarot Archetype:
The World
(Completion, integration, accomplishment, travel)

Tara #21 Praise:

Praise Her the One
Endowed with Calm Strength
Arrayed with the Three Truths of
Om Ah Hung
Vanquishing Demons
and All Who Give Harm
She is Ture,
Supreme and Unexcelled

Tara is the **completion of enlightenment,** the understanding that all is one. Nothing is separate from this unity. She has lifted all veils of illusion and doubt.

She is white, the color of space, of emptiness, of enlightenment. In this card, Her accents are purple, the color of the crown chakra and highest consciousness.

She sits atop a bull with golden hooves and horns, symbolic of steadfastness and power. Tara is completely in control of the most stubborn aspects of the mind. Her left leg is pulled in, for she has mastered the power of desire, and Her right leg is extended, for she is quick to go to all who call out to Her. This is just like the central #0 Tara of Wisdom, Compassion & Power. She holds Her right hand in the mudra of **protection** at Her heart, and in Her left hand she holds a trident, symbol of **the three jewels of Buddha, Dharma and sangha** (and also reinforcing the **three truths of "Om Ah Hung"** which manifest Her perfection of body, mind and spirit).

She is the only Tara seated with a moon behind Her head while also being surrounded by a garland of flames. She is the balance between sun and moon. Both are symbolic rather than literal, with the moon being prismatic and the flames being purple. They are beyond any reality we can understand.

She is one with the universe, and so she is surrounded by a galaxy of stars, connected to each one. A thousand-petaled lotus, symbol of the crown chakra, accents her number, 21. She is supreme, unexcelled, enlightened truth.

Tara #21 corresponds to the World card in the traditional tarot, which represents maturity and unity. This card is the completion of the journey of the Major Arcana. This Tara is the culmination of all. She is not young or old, but she is mature, capable, complete, nirvanic, all-knowing, and completely realized.

We each have within us all of the qualities of Tara, including complete enlightenment. In those moments of complete clarity, this Tara shines Her light through the illusions of suffering. We practice the dharma in order to find more of these moments of clarity and to bring these truths to others.

The lithomancy stone for complete enlightenment is **selenite**, sometimes called the "windowpane stone." This white, reflective stone is not clear. It can be helpful in cleansing space and connecting to the crown chakra.

PREMA'S COMMENTARY:

In the 21st Praise, we realize the fulfillment of all of Tara's qualities. We praise Her for integrating Body, Speech, and Mind. A Buddha is capable of having accurate perception in all the dimensions of consciousness.

The other thing this Praise reminds us is that even though Tara, as a Buddha, has manifested the fullness of enlightened mind, She still must be aware that negative demonic forces arise as long as She works within the realm of duality. She must be prepared to control these negative forces. In this way then, She is absolutely unexcelled, a Buddha, a fully awakened being.

Reflecting into the tarot card number 21: the World or the Universe. On this card we see a dancing female figure declaring fulfillment. Consciousness has reached its apex.

It has fully integrated all of its possibilities. So we wish for all beings that these praises will continue to inspire, and will call forth from each person the grace, the beauty, the wisdom, the compassion and the powerful skill and presence of the great Mother Tara.

Minor Arcana - Court Cards

The Major Arcana of 22 cards are important, but they are less than half of the deck. The remaining 56 cards are called the minor arcana. Traditionally separated into four suits of elemental cards, with four court (or "face") cards and ten elemental cards. These are similar to a regular deck of playing cards, separated into hearts (water), clubs (air), diamonds (earth), or spades (fire).

In a traditional tarot deck, the court cards are usually represented by royalty, like the King, Queen, Prince (sometimes Jack or Knight), and Princess. The face cards in a regular deck of playing cards are the King, Queen, and Jack (somehow the Princess was lost along the way).

In my deck, the court cards do not correspond directly to the four elemental suits. Rather, I used two other traditional Buddhist texts as inspiration for the sixteen court cards. Since they do not correspond directly, the order I present them in here does not particularly matter. They each have equal rank in their circles. None are higher "royalty" than another.

They are the "Protectors" of the Mandala. In the dance, Protector dancers draw a circle of protection around the dancers using the imagery of a vajra and a dorje, lightning and fire. They reflect all of the aspects of the 21 Taras through their dance.

The author dancing as Ferocious Compassion at the Tara Monlam in Brazil 2018. Photo credit to Dre Mendes.

Court Cards - Tara Tames the Eight Fears

One definition of Tara's name is "Rescuer." She immediately comes to the aid of all who call out to her. Many of her most well-known stories are called "Taming of the Eight Fears." Traditionally, it is said that any who call out to Tara for help will be saved by Her, though she may come in many different forms.

These are stories of Her protecting the Tibetan people from very real physical dangers, but the physical dangers represent inner harmful views that poison the mind. Through the dharma, we are given a way to tame the fear, an antidote to the poison.

These cards show Tara's antidote to each fear. Through practice, we can find equanimity and freedom in the midst of samsara.

I learned of Tara Tames the Eight Fears through a practice Prema primarily teaches to children, though the practice is quite profound for adults as well[1].

As part of the Mandala Dance practice, Prema also teaches the "Seven-branch prayer," a technique of purification to reveal the pure mind of Tara:

- ***We bow to purify arrogance***
- ***We offer to purify greed***
- ***We reveal all negativities to purify anger, hatred & war***
- ***We rejoice to purify jealousy***
- ***We request teachings to purify ignorance***
- ***We ask the Shining Ones to stay and purify our connection***
- ***We dedicate our practice to purify spiritual pride***

We each have the qualities of Tara within us, and the purifications help us to remember our own true nature. When these cards come up in a reading, I describe first the fear but also the antidote as wisdom for how to deal with it. We each have the power to face our fears.

Rejoicing Tames the Snakes of Jealousy

I call Mother Protector Tara,
Green as an emerald forest,
shining like a jewel
To teach me how to rejoice
for others' good fortune.
Mudita, sympathetic joy
Can save me from the snakes of jealousy.
The love of Tara tames all fears.

Jealousy is like a snake that strikes when we least expect it – when someone else gets the promotion or buys something we want. It just doesn't seem fair.

Jealousy also comes when something that we feel possessive of (like a partner or mate) shows that we truly cannot possess them by spending time or attention with someone else.

But by jealously holding tighter, we squeeze the life out of our partner just as surely as a boa constrictor. How can we tame the snake of jealousy?

The antidote is to **rejoice in the good fortune of others** (including the freedom of others to not be possessed by us). This is a challenging practice, but very powerful. It also can help remind us of how much great fortune we do have.

The card shows the image of Tara, Her right hand in the **mudra of protection** and Her left hand in the **mudra of refuge.** She is green in color for this fully enlightened activity. Only through rejoicing in others' good fortune can we find freedom from the snake of jealousy.

Forgiveness Tames the Fires of Anger

I call Mother Protector Tara,
White as the snow mountains,
shining like the sun,
To teach me how to forgive others and myself.
Revealing my own negativities
Can save me from the fires of anger.
The love of Tara tames all fears.

Fire is an incredibly volatile element, absolutely necessary to our survival but also incredibly dangerous and hard to control.

When anger arises, it can sometimes feel like burning fires, consuming all of our thoughts and actions.

We have a tendency to either strike out in anger, causing pain to others, or to turn our anger inward, causing pain to ourselves. When the fires of anger arise, and they always will, **offer compassion** to the person who is the source of your anger. Most of the time, people are not trying to make us angry. They are merely caught up in their own cycle of samsara, their own suffering and fear.

Forgiveness is like a healing balm on the painful burns that anger leaves. We can also only truly forgive when we "reveal our negativity," recognizing our own imperfections. How can we expect more of others than we are able to give ourselves?

The card shows the image of Tara, Her right hand in the **mudra of protection** and Her left hand in the **mudra of refuge**. She is white in color, healing and calming. Through forgiveness, we can find that control once again and tame the fires of anger.

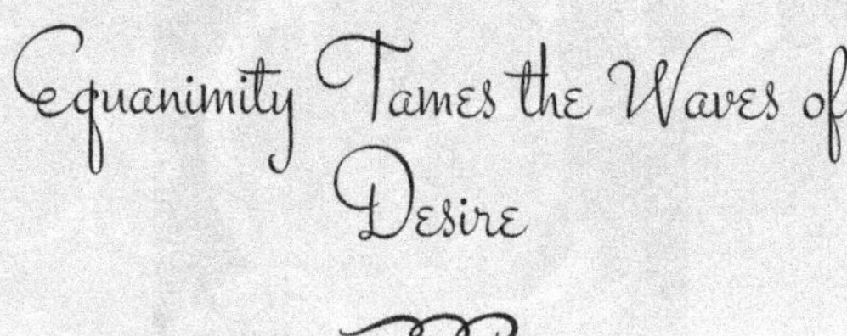

I call Mother Protector Tara,
Red as fire's dancing flames,
blazing like the sun,
To teach me how to find inner satisfaction
Equanimity, accepting all that comes,
Can save me from the waves of desire.
The love of Tara tames all fears.

Desire is a fundamental part of the human experience. We first experience desire as infants, wanting to be held, to be fed, to be comforted. As we grow, our desires also can grow, sometimes completely out of control.

We anesthetize ourselves with pleasure foods, clothing, gadgets, and more. And soon enough, our desire for these things can become stronger than our desire for freedom.

The waves hit harder when the things we desire are taken away from us. One of the primary sources of human suffering is loss of something we would prefer to keep.

This starts a cycle of frustration and fear as we struggle to maintain our desires. We can easily drown in this ocean. Tara's antidote is **equanimity**, which is mirrored in the waves themselves.

Things come. Things go. Moving in and out like the ocean waves, if we can meet our circumstances with equanimity, we can ride the waves rather than drowning in them.

The card shows the image of Tara, Her right hand in the **mudra of protection** and Her left hand in the **mudra of refuge**. She is red in color, magnetic and irresistible. By letting go we tame the waves of desire.

Generosity Tames the Prison of Greed

I call Mother Protector Tara,
Green as an emerald forest,
shining like a jewel,
To teach me how to give benefit to all.
Generously offering my good fortune
Can save me from the prison of greed.
The love of Tara tames all fears.

Greed is our tendency to cling and grasp to the things we have, whether they be possessions, people, or even circumstances. The very things we love become a prison. But Tara offers us the opportunity to escape this prison.

The antidote to greed is **generosity**. When we willingly offer all things precious to us, we receive manifold blessings. The greatest of these blessings is **freedom**.

Greed is different from desire because it is hoarding of what we have rather than wanting what we do not have. Even when living in physical poverty, we all have something to give.

Each of us has a **wealth of talents and gifts** that are as rich as any treasure. Are you willing to share your gifts? Your time and energy?

The card shows the image of Tara, Her right hand in the **mudra of protection** and Her left hand in the **mudra of refuge**, as she protects us from our own dangerous thought patterns. She is green in color, the image of enlightened mind.

Only through **sharing our good fortune** can we find true freedom from the chains of greed.

Mindfulness Tames the Elephants of Ignorance

I call Mother Protector Tara,
Yellow as the summer sun,
sparkling like a star
To teach me how to inspire my sluggish mind
Mindfulness of every single moment
Can save me from the elephants of ignorance.
The love of Tara tames all fears.

In Buddhism the elephant is a symbol of slow or sluggish mind. It is the tendency toward torpor or laziness. It is sometimes translated as "stupidity," but I believe that it's a more willful type of slow mind.

A person being trampled by the elephant of ignorance does not know or understand, but worse does not care about knowing or understanding. The antidote to this fear is consciousness.

The elephant in western imagery is also a symbol for memory, as elephants are said to have long memories. In Africa, they are seen as being a force stronger than nature. I will never forget the sign posted in Malawi, "Warning! Elephants have the right of way." Perhaps the elephant can serve as a reminder and a warning of how dangerous willful ignorance can be.

Through a diligent attempt to think and live consciously, we keep the elephants at bay. The card shows the image of Tara, Her right hand in the mudra of protection and Her left hand in the mudra of refuge, as she protects us from our own dangerous thought patterns. She is gold, the color of abundance, holding the elephant at bay through a generosity of will.

Humility Tames the Lions of Pride

I call Mother Protector Tara,
Blue as the deepest space, bright as the sky
To teach me how to tame my arrogance
Honoring the value of all beings
Can save me from the lions of pride.
The love of Tara tames all fears.

Pride is the tendency to set ourselves apart from others, forgetting about our interconnectedness. This concept of pride is like arrogance, when we we fail to recognize the value in others because of our own lack of confidence.

The antidote to pride is recognizing that all beings have infinite worth. Humility is not lowering one's self, but rather raising others up. There need not be groveling.

This extends to spiritual pride. We may find enlightenment and grow as spiritual leaders, but we also still have much to learn from others in our communities.

In the current deck this is listed as humility, but since this is somewhat confusing, this is one card I may change in the future. Another antidote to arrogance is self-confidence. When one is secure in their own abilities, there is no need to put down others.

The card shows the image of Tara, Her right hand in the mudra of protection and Her left hand in the mudra of refuge, as she protects us from our pride.

She is blue in color, ferocious and unwilling to put up with the silliness of egotism. Only through recognizing the value in all beings can we find freedom from the lion of pride.

Genuineness Tames the Thief of Wrong Ideas

I call Mother Protector Tara,
White as the snow mountains
shining like the sun
To teach me how to slow my monkey mind
Recognizing consequences of my actions
Can save me from the thief of wrong ideas.
The love of Tara tames all fears.

When we have a lack of understanding of consequence, we act on our wrong ideas. They creep into our lives in small ways – cheating on a test or telling little white lies.

Sometimes we lie to ourselves, preventing us from living authentic lives. But even these smallest deceptions steal from our integrity and virtue.

I chose to characterize the thief of wrong ideas as a monkey, the polar opposite of the elephants of ignorance (often called "monkey mind" and "elephant mind" in meditation practice). Elephants are too slow of mind, but monkey mind is too fast, never processing the consequences of actions.

Monkeys do often steal items from people – ask anyone who has hung laundry out to dry in a place with lots of monkeys. When we do not genuinely understand consequence, we are stealing from ourselves. Remembering the principle of karma, all actions will return. We know the right action to take.

The card shows the image of Tara, Her right hand in the mudra of protection and Her left hand in the mudra of refuge. She is white in color, healing and gentle. Only through genuineness can we find freedom from the monkey thief of wrong ideas.

Awareness Tames the Demons of Doubt

I call Mother Protector Tara,
Dark as volcanic rock, deep as the night sky
To teach me how to lift oppressive misery.
Awareness of my own true Buddha nature
Can save me from the demons of doubt.
The love of Tara tames all fears.

Whenever things don't go as we expect, doubt creeps in. Have I done something to cause my current negative circumstances? Am I just not good enough?

Doubt can lead to depression, which for some completely paralyzes the mind as if it is frozen in a glacier. And sometimes depression creeps in despite our life circumstances.

How can we thaw these doubts? Tara teaches us to do so through the pure light of awareness, recognizing our inherent worth and value as sentient beings.

She reminds us that we are each valuable and worthy of honor. This awareness breaks through the ice that has surrounded us, giving us hope. Even when all seems lost, this true nature glows at the heart of the ice.

The card shows the image of Tara, Her right hand in the mudra of protection and Her left hand in the mudra of refuge as she protects us from our doubt. She is black in color, ferocious and forceful in reminding us of our inherent worth.

The background of the card is a glacier, symbolizing the paralyzing nature of depression. The card is also accented with a question mark. Sometimes when teaching this system I have translated this part as the "Question of Doubt" rather than the "Demon," in order to strip away the connotation of religious language. We question ourselves, and it is only through awareness of our own value that we can we find freedom from doubt.

Court Cards - Auspicious Offering Goddesses

Part of the process of many Buddhist rituals is making offerings of some sort to the Buddhas and Bodhisattvas. These offerings sometimes manifest as physical objects. Other times a practitioner uses mudras, or sacred hand gestures. These offerings are elements of devotion and prayers.

On a cosmic level, many texts and artwork show seven or eight "Offering Goddesses." Often they are seen dancing and are called "Dakini," or "skydancer." Offering the physical or mudra offerings of these Goddesses is a powerful form of prayer.

I chose to base the second half of my court cards on dakinis offering the eight auspicious symbols, perhaps the best-known set of Buddhist symbols. They are painted on homes and used to decorate clothing and other items in many Tibetan communities. These symbols of good fortune were offered to Shakyamuni Buddha upon his enlightenment. As we all have within us the manifestations of the Buddhas, we each also have the offering of these symbols within.

I honestly did not know that the auspicious symbols were used in specific practices of Tara until well after I designed the deck. In his book *The Cult of Tara,* Stephen Beyer discusses many practices relating to Tara, including a set of prayers for goddesses offering the auspicious symbols. [1]

The colors for the dakinis on my cards do not correspond completely with the colors in Beyer's prayers, but I find these prayers beautiful and powerful in honoring the auspicious offerings. I will give my rationale in these pages.

My partner, Christopher Allen, and I adapted Beyer's prayers and set them to music with mudras in the song "May There Be Good Fortune." These are the versions of the prayers offered here. The song we wrote was recorded and can be downloaded on the Tara Dhatu website.

The Goddess Offers the Knot of Connection

May there be good fortune
By offering this holy object
Which sets the seal
of delight on the heart
Of the most noble
By this moonlike maiden
white as the snowy mountains,
proudly bearing aloft
the glorious knot of connection.

This offering Goddess is red as fire, presenting the immanent and irresistible truth that we are all infinitely interconnected to one another. Red is the color of magnetism and interconnectedness.

She is wearing a cream color. The knot continues over and under, with no beginning and never ending. Dagyab Rinpoche teaches, "The whole is comprised of a pattern closed in on itself with no gaps, which at once expresses motion and rest, all in a representational form of great simplicity and fully balanced harmony."[1]

A spider's web covered in dewdrops is woven through careful connections to become strong. The drops of dew are drops of the waters of compassion, woven throughout the interconnected web of life.

Through our interconnectedness, we understand that all of our gains and all of our losses belong to all sentient beings. We strive toward enlightenment for the sake of all. When this card arises in a reading, the Goddess is offering a chance to contemplate our connections, including how our actions may affect others.

The Goddess Offers the Wheel of Truth

May there be good fortune
By offering this holy object
Which sets the seal
of delight on the heart
Of the most noble
By this slender-bodied maiden,
Blazing with jasmine light,
Gracefully carrying
the golden wheel of truth.

This offering Goddess is green, representing enlightened activity, wearing gold, representing abundance and the jasmine light of Her prayer.

She is dancing, holding a wheel, symbolic of the dharmic understanding of truth. The wheel is in constant motion, changing and moving, but it is also grounded in substantial truth. Much like the knot, Dagyab Rinpoche describes the wheel as "all-embracing and complete in itself... at once in motion and at rest."[1]

The wheel represents the teachings. Buddhism holds great respect for the written word and the texts are considered to be sacred.

The background of this card shows the depths of caves within the earth. Many dharma teachings have been found or written in caves. Our ancestors depended on the cave as a source of shelter and therefore survival.

The cave represents the wisdom that rests deep within. When this card appears in a reading, the Goddess is offering a chance to understand or find a revelation of truth based on the wisdom of the past.

The Goddess Offers the Pure Lotus

May there be good fortune
By offering this holy object
Which sets the seal
of delight on the heart
of the most noble.
By this sixteen-year-old maiden,
Blazing with azure-blue light,
Coquettishly holding the precious
hundred-petaled lotus

This offering Goddess is white, as the purity of wisdom, adorned with the green of enlightened activity. She holds a rare blue lotus, emanating the azure-blue light of Her prayer. The lotus grows out of the mud, muck and mire in its purity and beautiful form. It represents the blossoming of auspicious activities and is the ground on which the deities rest (sitting upon the lotus).

The lotus is innately feminine, a potent metaphor for female sexuality.

Tara is called the "lotus-born one" for in the story she arose out of a lotus formed in a pool of the tears of compassion. Every form of the major arcana of Tara sits or stands upon a lotus.

When this card appears in a reading, the Goddess is offering a chance to make the most out of a difficult situation, a chance for grounding, growth and transformation.

The Goddess Offers the Banner of Victory

May there be good fortune
By offering this holy object
Which sets the seal
of delight on the heart
of the most noble
By the victorious pale-green maiden,
Learn'ed in amorous melody,
Singing Her deep-throated tones
as she raises the banner of victory.

The gold Goddess wearing purple reflects Tara #4, All Victorious. She radiates abundance and regal mastery, a true victory over samsara.

The banner of victory was raised by the Buddha on the top of Mount Meru after he defeated armies of confusion. It represented the triumph of knowledge over ignorance and death.

According to Dagyab Rinpoche, the banner represents "the victory of knowledge over ignorance or the victory over all hindrances, the attainment of happiness."[1]

So you may raise your banner high to celebrate your accomplishments, your wisdom, and what you have to offer. The sunset represents completion of the cycle.

When this card arises in a reading, the Goddess is offering an opportunity to overcome whatever obstacles are preventing true victory over ego and desire. It is also an opportunity to share with others about your accomplishments.

The Goddess Offers the Parasol of Protection

May there be good fortune
By offering this holy object
Which sets the seal
of delight on the heart
Of the most noble
By this long-eyed maiden,
the color of powdered vermillion,
shooting arrows of Her glance
as she twirls the parasol of protection.

This offering Goddess is white, offering a calm peace, and wears a deep vermillion red, magnetic with Her inevitability.

She offers the parasol, an ancient symbol of protection from the fierce sun. The sun is brilliant, but even sunshine burns when you get too much. The coolness of the parasol's shade offers protection from suffering, desire, obstacles, illnesses and harmful forces.

The parasol also represents nobility, for in many cultures, only a powerful person of high stature would have the luxury of a parasol. According to Dagyab Rinpoche, the parasol represents spiritual power.

When this card arises in a reading, the Goddess is offering a cool place to rest in refuge from harm. Yet this refuge also takes effort and a willingness to let go of the things we so often grasp that cause us harm.

Gather around you that which can shelter you and protect you from harm. Alternatively, perhaps you are being called upon to give protection.

The Goddess Offers the Vase of Treasure

May there be good fortune
By offering this holy object
Which sets the seal of delight on the heart
Of the most noble
By this shapely maiden,
White as clouds on the horizon,
Enticingly holding in her hand the vase of treasure.

The golden Goddess offers a vase of treasure, symbolic of the womb of life. She is abundance manifest. She wears pale blue, color of the clouds in the sky as they gather to pour forth Her rains.

A large, wish-fulfilling jewel tops the vase, indicating it is "the inexhaustible vessel... a sign of the fulfillment of spiritual and material wishes."[1]

In its pure symbolic form, the treasure vase is said to hold the waters of longevity, and treasure vases are often placed or buried in springs, rivers and oceans to spread abundance in the environment.

The water falls as a drop, which ripples out infinitely, just as compassion begins with one drop and changes the world. This Goddess is raining treasure upon us and sustaining life.

When this card arises in a reading, take a moment to reflect on the abundance that sustains your life. This is the treasure that is offered.

The Goddess Offers the Conch of Sound

May there be good fortune
By offering this holy object
Which sets the seal
of delight on the heart
Of the most noble
By this glorious maiden,
The color of stainless emerald,
Seductively grasping
the right-handed
conch of sound.

The green Goddess of air offers the conch shell, a symbol of the teachings of the Buddha which travel through the invisible means of sound. She is enlightened activity wrapped in the powerful purple.

Just as a conch is used as a horn to proclaim victory, it also is used in rituals to remind us of the sound of victory over suffering. As a symbol, it represents "the fame of the Buddha's teaching, which spreads in all directions like the sound of the conch trumpet."[1]

The background of this card shows the colors of the aurora borealis, the natural phenomenon named after Goddess of the dawn and the north wind.

These lights are impermanent, but they draw others through their beauty and presence, much like the sound of the conch travels through the wind and calls others to listen.

When this card arises in a reading, the Goddess offers a call to awaken and work for the benefit of others.

The Goddess Offers the Fish of Freedom

May there be good fortune
By offering this holy object
Which sets the seal
of delight on the heart
Of the most noble
By this ravishing maiden,
Pleasing as a peacock,
Flashing like lightning
as she holds the fish of freedom.

The double fish represent freedom and fluidity due to their ability to move freely in water. They can not only move forward and back, but up and down. They are characterized by their fluidity.

As they are golden in color, they also represent abundance and prosperity. The greatest gift of physical prosperity is the freedom to share generously.

This offering Goddess is a pale blue, pleasing as a peacock, with white clothes symbolic of healing and peace.

When this card arises in a reading, the Goddess is offering an opportunity to remain flexible and stay in motion, regardless of how turbulent the waters may have become.

Freedom comes through spontaneity. This is a true source of happiness.

Minor Arcana - Elemental Suits

The remaining minor arcana are based on traditional tarot meanings of the minor arcana from a dharma perspective. As in tarot, the minor arcana are separated into the four elements of Earth, Air, Water and Fire.

I have chosen Buddhist ritual tools which correspond loosely with the traditional magical tools of Tarot. The suits are: Earth (Wheels/Discs), Fire (Vajras/Swords), Water (Vases/Cups) and Air (Bells/Wands). Under each "Tarot Archetype," I listed the traditional meaning of that card. These were the inspiration I considered when creating the minor arcana.

The aces of the suits are Manifestation (Wheels), Wisdom (Bells), Compassion (Vases), and Power (Vajras). Tara calls us to manifest wisdom, compassion, and power. This is the essence of the elements and the essence of dharma practice.

Element of Space

In addition to these four elements, Tibetan Buddhism includes a fifth element of Space. Space surrounds and permeates all things. At the atomic level, we are each made up primarily of..... space.

There is not a suit for space in the minor arcana of this deck, but the words on each card are white, the color of space.

Allowing space in our lives for things to unfold as they will, equanimity for whatever comes, gives us an opportunity for peace in the midst of challenges.

Suit of Wheels: Element of Earth

In Buddhism, the color for the element of Earth is gold, the color of abundance. The Earth brings form to matter and manifestation of substance. It is a place of grounding and stability, just like our planet Earth. Yet it is also constantly in motion, spinning around the sun and on its own axis.

The symbol for the suit of Earth in this deck is the wheel, constantly in motion. Impermanence is the only constant.

The Dharma of truth is usually represented by a wheel with eight spokes, representing the Eightfold Path:

- Right View,
- Right Intent,
- Right Speech,
- Right Action,
- Right Livelihood,
- Right Effort,
- Right Mindfulness, and
- Right Concentration.

~

The Wheels in this Deck:

Ace of Wheels: Manifestation
Two of Wheels: Duality
Three of Wheels: Diligence
Four of Wheels: Attachment
Five of Wheels: Affliction
Six of Wheels: Benefit
Seven of Wheels: Patience
Eight of Wheels: Impermanence
Nine of Wheels: Increase
Ten of Wheels: Mastery

Ace of Wheels: Manifestation

Tarot Archetype: Ace of Discs
(Reward, Manifestation)

The path of manifestation takes an idea and brings it into physical form.

Just as the flowers in the card's background have been cultivated to blossom, so we have the potential to cultivate manifestation of abundance in our lives.

Yet, if a shadow is planted, it will also grow. What have you planted? What will you grow?

Will you manifest the qualities of Wisdom, Compassion, and Power?

Or will you cultivate ignorance, selfishness, and pain?

How can you bring the most benefit into the world?

The physical world is often associated with the root chakra, physical form, the body, and health. But the wheel is unstable, always moving and changing. We exist in this world of physical form.

Manifestation cannot happen by accident. You must cultivate the qualities purposefully and with intention, for the sake of all beings.

Two of Wheels: Duality

Tarot Archetype: Two of Discs
(Change, Balance)

The zebra's black and white stripes seem to be a pattern of opposites, the polarity of light and dark, but actually they act as camouflage. When a herd of zebras runs together, it is difficult for predators to pick one out of the herd.

Duality is our tendency of seeing ourselves as separate from one another, the whole "us" against "them" philosophy.

It is by understanding our interconnectedness with all of life that we can turn from the dance of duality. We need not be separate from one another at all. We are, in fact, infinitely interconnected.

How do you hold yourself separate? How do you see yourself as more or less than another?

Are you seeing a situation as black and white when it would be better to find one of the many shades of gray?

Three of Wheels: Diligence

Tarot Archetype: Three of Discs
(Work, Completion)

Diligence is persistence through all obstacles, the willingness to work hard to accomplish a goal. Yet, it is also consciousness, paying attention to the details along the way.

In order to climb a mountain, persistence and attention to detail is essential. In order to attain an enlightened state of mind, one must diligently practice the dharma and live in a conscious way. So many obstacles appear, but through diligence we can overcome all obstacles.

What is your obstacle? Can you see your goal? How can you be more persistent toward your goal?

"Through the diligence of our practice is the pure dharma spread..." - The Tara Mandala Dance Practice

---

Four of Wheels: Attachment

Tarot Archetype: Four of Discs
(Avarice, Consuming)

There are two causes of suffering in life, attachment and aversion. Aversion is avoidance of "bad" things we fear. Attachment is attempt to keep the "good" things we have. Equanimity is the practice of seeing things as neither good nor bad, but merely what they are.

When you become attached to an idea, object, or person, that attachment causes you to lose sight of its true nature. Often, the object of attachment is lost along the way.

These things may be precious to you, like the golden citrine is a precious gemstone representing wealth, but attachment will consume you if you are not conscious of it.

What is holding you back? There are always things we fear to lose. Whether you see them as good attachments or negative, all attachments ultimately lead to suffering.

Five of Wheels: Affliction

Tarot Archetype: Five of Discs
(Hardship, Affliction)

Sometimes the greatest obstacle is not the boulder before you, but the pebble in your shoe. We all carry burdens, some great and some small.

The small afflictions can be like tiny rocks that are hard to walk on barefoot. They make your path so much more difficult. Individually they may not be so bad, but collectively, they cause great hardship.

These become baggage or difficulty, especially if you pick them up and carry them. Soon they are no longer small rocks. Why are you carrying such big, heavy rocks?

How can you release the afflictions that burden you?

How can you protect yourself from walking on the rocks?

Affliction
Five of Wheels

Six of Wheels: Benefit

Tarot Archetype: Six of Discs
Charity, Generosity

Fruit is the generosity of the earth, bringing forth sweet abundance to spread seeds and begin a new cycle of growth. What fruit do you have to share from your own garden? What seeds will you plant?

When the fruit begins to blossom, how will you recognize that it is ready to harvest? Are you paying attention?

The purpose of spiritual practice is to bring benefit to others. It is not appropriate to keep all of the fruit of your spiritual practice for yourself alone.

As you have manifested great benefit in your life, how will you share it? This may be material wealth. It may be a spiritual harvest.

Whatever your great wealth is, you have so much. You cannot use all of it yourself. That is not how it works.

If you hoard your fruit and refuse to share, it will inevitably rot. If you are generous with the fruit, you will easily cultivate more.

You have enough and to share. Be diligent in your generosity. Give more than you take. And your harvest will be plentiful.

~

~

Seven of Wheels: Patience

Tarot Archetype: Seven of Discs
(Failure, Patience)

Have patience. It did not happen quickly, whatever it is.

The tree takes the time necessary to plant roots and gather nutrients before it tries to stand up tall. It does not hurry.

Strength is cultivated through patience, the willingness to slow down and build things correctly from the roots up.

You can build strong, intricate roots in your life if you are willing to do so slowly, one step at a time.

The roots are your sources of Refuge, the dharma, sangha, and Buddha. The branches are the benefit you share with all beings.

Patience
Seven of Wheels

Eight of Wheels: Impermanence

Tarot Archetype: Eight of Discs
(Protection, Contentment)

The wheels turn, just as the world is constantly in a state of transition.

Change is the only absolute constant. The card shows autumn leaves just as they are beginning to change colors, surrounded by green.

The leaves will soon die, but that is part of the cycle.

So the circumstances in your life will change, and then change again, and then change again, and so on.

Release attachment to find contentment, regardless of the circumstances.

Impermanence
Eight of Wheels

Nine of Wheels: Increase

Tarot Archetype: Nine of Discs
(Accomplishment)

In tropical climates, the plants grow higher and higher, reaching ever toward the warmth of the sun.

You also can grow beyond your wildest imagination, but you must start small and build upon a firm foundation, both in the spiritual and material realms.

Of all cards in the Suit of Earth, this card is the most related to physical manifestation, an abundance of wealth.

Your efforts will pay off. You may have to dip down a bit before you can rise (see how the first few wheels drop lower?).

It may seem like things will never get better. They most assuredly will.

Increase
Nine of Wheels

Ten of Wheels: Mastery

Tarot Archetype: Ten of Discs
Learning, Productivity

You have achieved mastery over part of your life, a peak experience. Yet you must not become complacent about your mastery, for even a master craftsperson must continue the craft to keep the skills.

Take healthy pride in your work thus far, but recognize that the work has only just begun.

Sometimes you find yourself balancing what feels like too many plates in the air. You can do it, just as nine of these wheels balance on the one. You have mastery over the situation.

But as the wheels are constantly in motion, you cannot maintain the balance forever. When you lose balance, do not despair. Find mastery in the valleys as well as the peaks.

"Just as treasures are uncovered from the earth, so virtue appears from good deeds, and wisdom appears from a pure and peaceful mind. To walk safely through the maze of human life, one needs the light of wisdom and the guidance of virtue." – Shakyamuni Buddha

---

1

Suit of Bells: Element of Air

The color for the element of Air is green, the color of enlightened activity. Green is also the color of the heart chakra, also associated with air.

When we breathe in air, it fills our heart chakra. We breathe out wisdom and compassion as we open to the world. Mind training is the source of enlightenment.

All things arise within the mind. The seat of the mind is not just the brain, but also in the heart.

The mind is everything. What you think you become. - The Buddha

---

In this deck, the suit of air is represented by the bell of emptiness and sound, as it is the emptiness of the "cup" of the bell that allows for its resonant sound.

The teachings of the dharma travel through sound, which is associated with air.

~

Ace of Bells: Wisdom
Two of Bells: Balance
Three of Bells: Fears
Four of Bells: Refuge
Five of Bells: Dangers
Six of Bells: Concentration
Seven of Bells: Mystery
Eight of Bells: Freedom
Nine of Bells: Illusion
Ten of Bells: Emptiness

Ace of Bells: Wisdom

Tarot Archetype: Ace of Wands
(Thought, Doom)

All things arise within the mind. While the realm of thought may be comparative to doom in the Western tarot, in the dharma the highest level of mind is wisdom.

Wisdom, compassion and power are the attributes of green central Tara, and they are each necessary to balance the others. Wisdom without compassion results in cold-hearted intellectualism, while compassion without wisdom can lead to painful vulnerability.

Either without power is merely ineffectual. The three must be cultivated together.

I adorned this ace card with an owl. These birds are symbolic of a longing to know and understand the world and, by extension, the true nature of reality.

Wisdom
Ace of Bells

Two of Bells: Balance

Tarot Archetype: Two of Wands
(Balance)

Balance is of utmost importance when walking the Middle Way, the balance between aestheticism and excess.

Just as the two sides of the butterfly balance in symmetry, allowing the magnificent creature to fly and land on tiny feet, there are two sides to every situation.

Just as the breath comes in, so it goes out. Find balance rather than duality by recognizing the other as a mirror.

Like the butterfly, you must let go of your past self as a caterpillar in order to find your future self as a butterfly.

Balance
Two of Bells

Three of Bells: Fears

Tarot Archetype: Three of Wands
(Sorrow, Distress)

Some days the storm clouds gather and threaten to rain, but the result is not yet inevitable. Fears creep into our minds and sometimes take over, and these fears are often not based in what will happen but merely in what might happen.

Besides, in a drought, the rain is a blessing, not a curse.

So whatever your fear, try to keep in in perspective. It may feel huge, but these are small sorrows, small moments of distress.

These clouds are dark, but all is not lost.

May all fears and all dangers be removed and dispelled!

Fears
Three of Bells

Four of Bells: Refuge

Tarot Archetype: Four of Wands
(Seclusion, Inner Strength)

When the light breaks through a dense patch of clouds, creating the proverbial silver lining, remember that all is not lost. This image represents the light of the true refuge heart, the sparkling gem found deep within.

This light of Tara resonates with the light in the heart center of others, reaffirming our connection. It is as if love breaks through the darkest of clouds.

Sometimes you must go into seclusion to find inner strength, but true refuge comes through connection to others.

Refuge
Four of Bells

Five of Bells: Dangers

Tarot Archetype: Five of Wands
(Defeat, Opposition)

Unlike the clouds in the "Fears" card (Three of Bells), in this case it is definitely going to rain. Danger is imminent. But, again, you have a choice in how you will meet that danger.

Will you meet it with wisdom, compassion and power, or will you meet it with fear?

Tara gives us the strength to break through all obstacles. All fears and all dangers are removed and dispelled when we call on that strength.

What do the darkest of storm clouds bring? Rain. And perhaps thunder and lightning. Let the storm come.

Open yourself to your biggest fears. They exist. They aren't going to go away.

Then, what happens next. For there is always a next.

Six of Bells: Concentration

Tarot Archetype: Six of Wands
(Safe, Passage)

Sand mandalas are large, intricate, and detailed works of art made out of colored sand that take days for Buddhist monks to complete.

When finished, the mandala is destroyed in a ritual action of blowing the sands away. This represents the transitory nature of existence.

The concentration necessary to create the mandala exists in the present moment, not the future.

In order to find safe passage through danger, one must concentrate on only the present moment. How can you concentrate your current endeavors?

Take time. Take a breath. Breathe in. And out.

And again. Breathe in.

. . .

And out.

And again.

Breathe in. And Out.

Concentrate.

Good. Keep breathing.

~

~

Seven of Bells: Mystery

Tarot Archetype: Seven of Wands
(Disillusion, Bondage)

As long as we live in the world of samsara, there are aspects of the true nature of reality that remain mysterious, as if in a fog.

This is a type of bondage, keeping us from finding our true path. Seek to break the illusion and clear away the mystery in order to find your way.

Yet the breaking of illusion need not be disillusionment.

There is no need to be disappointed, but merely to recognize the illusory nature of reality. By recognizing it, you needn't be bound by it.

This card always reminds me of one of my favorite quotes from a movie, *Shakespeare in Love*. "How's it going to end? I don't know. It's a mystery." That's pretty much life, isn't it?

As soon as we think we have it all figured out, that's when we figure out all the stuff we don't have figured out.

~

~

Eight of Bells: Freedom

Tarot Archetype: Eight of Wands
(Opposition, Unstable Action)

Just as a bird in flight represents freedom, so you have the ability to free your mind from attachment and illusion.

You must let go of the ground if you truly want to fly. It must be terrifying to let go of the ground the first time.

You also might meet resistance, just as the bird meets wind resistance.

Much of our resistance we provide ourselves. It takes diligence and patience to be truly free.

Are you looking for freedom in this situation? Hoping for it? Or do you already have it? Do you want or need it?

Freedom
Eight of Bells

Nine of Bells: Illusion

Tarot Archetype: Nine of Wands
(Cruelty, Punishing)

The cruelest aspect of the phenomenal world is the illusion that everything is solid and clear when really we build our lives on a foundation of clouds.

Folk singer Joni Mitchell famously mused about clouds as an illusion:

So many things I would have done
But clouds got in my way
I've looked at clouds from both sides now
From up and down and still somehow
It's cloud illusions I recall
I really don't know clouds at all[1]

While it may look solid, it is merely an illusion. The solidity of this world is no more real than the layer of clouds.

Or is it an illusion that the clouds are not solid? Can it be both?

What are the illusions in your life?

Break through the illusion to see things as they really are.

Ten of Bells: Emptiness

Tarot Archetype:
Ten of Wands
Ruin, Shattered Delusions

While emptiness in the Western world is often seen from an extremely negative perspective (and the traditional meaning of this card is negative), in Buddhism emptiness is one of the manifestations of true enlightened mind.

When we can move past our illusions and delusions and let go of our obstacles and fears, we can allow our minds to experience the expansive blue sky of infinite space.

Form is emptiness. Emptiness is form. According to the Wisdom of Air, our emptiness is truly full.

"To enjoy good health, to bring true happiness to one's family, to bring peace to all, one must first discipline and control one's own mind. If a man can control his mind he can find the way to Enlightenment, and all wisdom and virtue will naturally come to him." – *Shakyamuni Buddha*[1]

Suit of Vases: Element of Water

The color for the element of Water is blue, the color of discipline. Water moves with fluidity, but it also must be held within a container like a vase.

Water is associated with emotions, which may feel out of control. But with disciplined practice, emotions can be powerful tools.

Ace of Vases: Compassion
Two of Vases: Connection
Three of Vases: Becoming
Four of Vases: Offerings
Five of Vases: Suffering
Six of Vases: Remembrance
Seven of Vases: Creativity
Eight of Vases: Devotion
Nine of Vases: Reflection
Ten of Vases: Fulfillment

"Drop by drop is the water pot filled. Likewise, the wise man, gathering it little by little, fills himself with good." - The Buddha

---

Ace of Vases: Compassion

Tarot Archetype: Ace of Cups
(Feeling, Love)

As with the other aces, Compassion is one of the primary aspects of central Tara. It is one of Her strongest qualities.

This type of compassion does not refer to pity or sympathy, but rather fully recognizing the needs of others. From great social justice projects to simple kindnesses, acts and thoughts of compassion change the world.

When we act with compassion, it is as if we are dropping a stone into a pool of still water, creating ripples from that drop that reverberate infinitely. One compassionate act begets another.

Self-compassion is just as important as compassion for others. We live in a world of self-criticism and judgment. Remember to be gentle with yourself.

All dharma practice is rooted in compassion, for we are concerned not only about material needs but also the need to be free from attachment and aversion. The prayer "May all beings be happy. May all beings be free" sends our compassionate wishes into the world.

~

~

Two of Vases: Connection

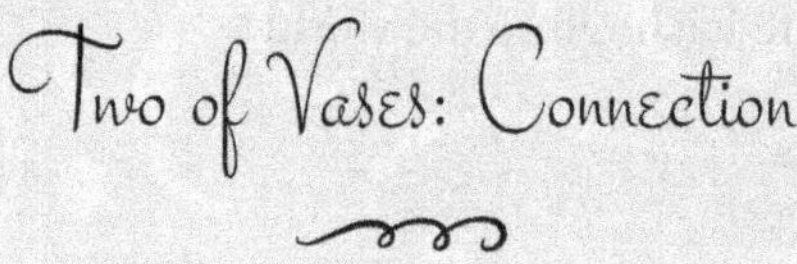

Tarot Archetype: Two of Cups
(Romance, Reciprocity)

Bridges have long been considered magical, bringing together two worlds. It is a place of transition, a place of connection.

Bridges are also a magical place of in-between, neither here nor there. When you are on a bridge, you are suspended in liminal space.

I remember reading a "choose your own adventure" book as a child about a tunnel or bridge that I think about often when I'm driving. In that book, the characters time-traveled when they went across a bridge. I cannot help but think about it every time I cross a bridge now. What am I going to find on the other side?

What is bridging in your life? Are there bridges you need to build, connections you need to make?

Or do you need to recognize a connection you already have?

Remember the interconnectedness of all existence. Every person has infinite connections to all that exists. We have a vital responsibility to recognize and act on this interconnected through our wisdom, compassion, and power.

What about burned bridges? Have there been connections that went sour in your life, difficult or toxic relationships that need healing? What resources do you need to approach these bridges again? Or is it healthier for you to stay away?

What bridges will you build?

~

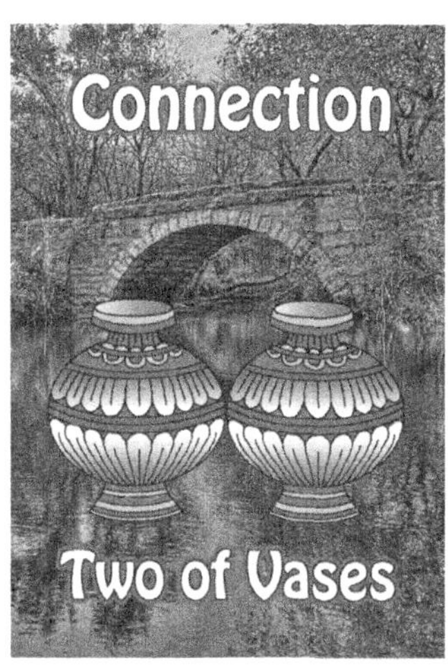

~

Three of Vases: Becoming

Tarot Archetype: Three of Cups
(Grace, Fraternity)

In the winter, water turns solid into ice and it seems that life will end. But by grace, the snow melts, becoming something new, fluid, and magnificent.

This card shows the moment of transition, the very end of the winter, when the freeze begins to thaw. You can see movement for the first time.

It's a brilliant beginning and opening. Life can move. You are no longer paralyzed with indecision. Now you will get momentum.

An object at rest will remain at rest, but an object in motion will catapult at light speed. Be prepared for things to take off much more quickly than you could possibly expect.

What is opening up and coming into being for you right now? Are there areas of your life that seemed frozen but now are beginning to thaw?

Pay attention to the changes, that which is becoming. There is movement and rushing water even in the midst of the snow.

And it's going to rush into springtime before you know it.

Also be aware of the light shining on the ice as it melts, as it could dazzle you. Be careful. Melting snow and ice can be fun and amazing, but it also can be dangerous.

~

~

Four of Vases: Offerings

Tarot Archetype: Four of Cups
(Decline, Opportunity)

Water is often an offering given on Buddhist altars and in sacred springs. These offerings pour out in abundance, creating opportunities for powerful blessings.

Rather than declining, an offering freely given multiplies as it pours out, just as these waterfalls multiply over the cliffs.

The most common offering made in Buddhist rituals is an offering of seven bowls of water in order to cultivate generosity. Water is offered because generosity should be given freely, just as water is freely available in Tibet.

Think about the resources you have. What do you do with them? Do you hold them close and keep them to yourself? Do you have a perspective of scarcity? Or do you think about how you can give to others?

What do you have to give? It does not have to be an offering of material goods. Maybe your offering will be time or talent. Or perhaps you will be called to give a portion of your manifested material abundance.

What offering can you make? Will you give freely and generously?

~

~

Five of Vases: Suffering

Tarot Archetype: Five of Cups
Regret, Disillusionment

The sea of suffering is fraught with dangers and despair. There is no illusion of safety.

Suffering arises naturally as part of samsara, the cycle of death and rebirth to which life in the material world is bound. It is so easy to get stuck in the midst of it, seeing no way out.

When you only see the storm from within the chaos, how can there be anything else? It seems utterly hopeless at times.

How can you manage until the storm passes?

Can you release the two causes of suffering, attachment and aversion? Can you let go?

This is a difficult card to get in a reading, no matter what the placement. And yet, it is a realistic card, for we all experience suffering in every aspect of our lives.

The purpose of spiritual practice is to root out the causes and to find methods of release.

May all beings be free from suffering and the causes of suffering.

~

~

Six of Vases: Remembrance

Tarot Archetype: Six of Cups
Childhood, Nostalgia

Waves come in and out, in and out. If you stay too long in one place, your feet get stuck in the sand.

Sometimes it is fun to look back, and reflection and remembrance can be healthy.

But if you watch, remember, and keep moving, you can find peace within the constant flow of the ocean.

Equanimity is the goal. Stay in motion.

Think of the past. Remember. Think of the future. All time exists within this present moment.

Remembrance
Six of Vases

Seven of Vases: Creativity

Tarot Archetype: Seven of Cups
Dream, Imagination

Human beings are rarely content to build things that are simply practical. We look for form, color, light, and shape... we look for beauty. Just as sea creatures built this coral reef as their habitat, so you may feel the need to create beauty instead of just function.

While the word creativity often brings to mind visual art, music, dance, theatre, and other art forms, the power to create comes in many shapes and forms, not just "artistic" abilities.

Creativity is the ability to imagine things to be different from the way they currently are.

Tara of Creative Wisdom helps us find new and different ways of dealing with obstacles. You have the ability to do many things in your own unique way. You are the only person capable of creating exactly in your style. Listen to your creative voice. Be willing to speak. Use that voice chakra.

The coral reef once was one thing and now is something else entirely. Learn to look at things from another point of view.

~

~

Eight of Vases: Devotion

Tarot Archetype: Eight of Cups
Loss, Letting Go

Life is full of loss. One of the primary sources of suffering is our aversion to this loss. It can be difficult to make your way through the swamp of sadness.

It's easy to let the murkiness bog you down into some level of desperation. But if you maintain devotion to your right intentions and let go of your expectations, you can survive and even thrive.

This card is actually a very positive card. While it is a swamp, it is a thriving ecosystem. All of the wildlife work together in symbiotic harmony. If you remain devoted to your practice, you can also find harmony.

What harmony are you seeking in your life? What devotion is needed?

Devotion
Eight of Vases

Nine of Vases: Reflection

Tarot Archetype: Nine of Cups
(Happiness, Well-being)

Julian of Norwich said, "All will be well, and all will be well, and all manner of things will be well." Water is so often in movement, but when still it is an opportunity a mirror of reflection.

Regardless of your circumstances, in the depth of the still pool you have opportunity to reflect on what brings you deep and abiding peace.

Take the moments of stillness.

Breathe.

Pause.

. . .

And move forward.

Ten of Vases: Fulfillment

Tarot Archetype: Ten of Cups
(Salvation, Joyful Attainment)

Out of the depths of murky water, the lotus grows and blossoms, a fulfillment of potential and possibility.

Though many flowers grow through the water, the lotus is the only one with a stalk firm enough to rise above the surface of the water. Yet a lotus grows out of murky, dark water. What are your dark waters? Have you dealt with the challenges?

This is a joyful attainment of potential. All of life's experiences have prepared you for this moment.

Think about the difficulties you have overcome. What is ready to blossom in your life?

"You can search throughout the entire universe for someone who is more deserving of your love and affection than you are yourself, and that person is not to be found anywhere. You yourself, as much as anybody in the entire universe deserve your love and affection." – Shakyamuni Buddha[1]

Suit of Vajras: Element of Fire

The color for the element of Fire is red, the color of magnetism. Fire draws us to its warmth, but its power can destroy if not used properly.

The tool of fire, the vajra, in Sanskrit is translated "thunderbolt" or "diamond." It is a ritual implement used to generate metaphysical power. It symbolizes the male principle while the bell symbolizes the female principle.

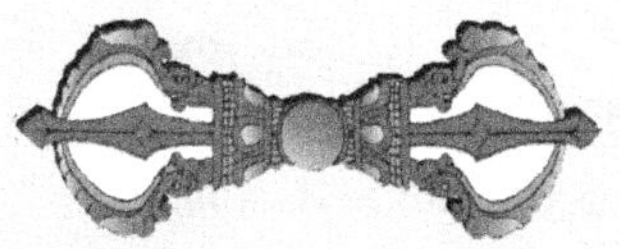

The two objects are often found together in Tibetan rituals. In this deck, Wisdom (the bell) and Power (the vajra) balance each other. Air is the mind, the initial thought. Fire is the spark, the catalyst that inspires action.

Ace of Vajras: Power
Two of Vajras: Alliance
Three of Vajras: Will
Four of Vajras: Completion
Five of Vajras: Obstacles
Six of Vajras: Empowerment
Seven of Vajras: Confidence
Eight of Vajras: Destruction
Nine of Vajras: Protection
Ten of Vajras: Magnetism

"Everything You Need Is Already Inside You Don't Wait For Others To Light Your Fire You Have Your Own Matches" - Darren Hardy

---

Ace of Vajras: Power

Tarot Archetype: One of Swords
(Power)

Tara manifests in Her central form as Wisdom, Compassion and Power, the three aces of Air, Water and Fire. Thus, power is central to Her form. Tara's power emanates from the source of all power in the universe. It is radiant energy made form. This is not power over but power through all beings.

It connects to the energy at the core of all life. This raw, pure power must be directed to bring about benefit. In the card, this is shown through the power of sunlight through the trees.

The sun gives us warmth, heat and energy, and gives us the potential for growth and survival.

Power
Ace of Vajras

Two of Vajras: Alliance

Tarot Archetype: Two of Swords
(Alliance, Vision)

An alliance is a bringing together of energies. When two people ally themselves, they bring their will into accord with one another. Though they may seem to be moving in different directions, they are connected at their source or the alliance is sure to fail.

Another name for the vajra is the dorje, and two vajras together form another symbol called the double-dorje.

Just as the rays of the sun seem to be traveling in many directions, they all begin at their connection to one another. Choose your alliances carefully, and when you do build them, make sure to keep the connections true.

Alliance
Two of Vajras

Three of Vajras: Will

Tarot Archetype:
Three of Swords
(Fate, Will)

What do you will into being? Will is the determination and power to make something happen, and it is incredibly important to align personal will with greater will.

This is why we dedicate our practice to the benefit of all beings. We do not practice merely for personal gain.

Will is also about focus and concentration, just as the candle flame is a concentrated source of power.

Is your will in alignment? Take charge and follow through.

Will
Three of Vajras

Four of Vajras: Completion

Tarot Archetype:
Four of Swords
(Success, Completion)

The day has passed; the job is done. As the sun sets, there is a sense of finishing and completion. What was set in motion has come to pass.

While this does lead to a period of darkness (and rest), it is time to honor the accomplishments you have reached.

This may be a graduation, of sorts. An ending, or closure. It feels full and good. You finished. You did the work. You are ready to move on to something new.

Completion
Four of Vajras

Five of Vajras: Obstacles

Tarot Archetype: Five of Swords
(Impasse, Conflict)

Obstacles are inevitable in the realm of samsara, as we are constantly in conflict with ourselves and others. When you meet an obstacle, how do you face it?

Do you hide it deep down inside where it will burn from the inside out? Or do you lash out, causing damage to others?

If you aren't careful, the obstacles can overcome you. However, a controlled burn can actually bring fertility to the land, and obstacles can make us stronger.

In the purifications, we reveal our own negativities to purify anger, hatred and war. How can this help when you face obstacles?

And never forget, fire can be dangerous. Really, really dangerous.

Obstacles
Five of Vajras

Six of Vajras: Empowerment

Tarot Archetype: Six of Swords
(Glory, Victory)

You are made of the same stuff as stars, infinitely beautiful in your shining, sparkling light. Allow the recognition of your own true nature to empower you as you embody your own true Tara nature.

Just as the water reflects the light of the star, you can reflect the inherent light you find within yourself. Allow this to be a guide to where you need to go.

Find your way back to your own inherent worth. You are light. You are magical. You are wonder. You are a radiant being, interconnected with all.

Empowerment
Six of Vajras

Seven of Vajras: Confidence

Tarot Archetype: Seven of Swords
(Challenge, Courage)

Just as the Tara of Invincible Courage gives us confidence to face unknown obstacles, you have the power to meet your challenges with courage.

The bearded dragon is a symbol of standing up in the face of challenges. Like all lizards, it can sense even the tiniest vibrations in the earth.

Thus it can quickly detect both predators and prey. This knowledge allows it to move with great speed, either in defense or attack, and this is a matter of survival.

Confidence in yourself and in your own intuition will allow you to make decisions. Hold your head high as you listen to the wisdom within.

Confidence
Seven of Vajras

Eight of Vajras: Destruction

Tarot Archetype: Eight of Swords
(Fall, Swiftness)

If left uncontrolled, fire can cause an extreme amount of sheer destruction, as shown in this forest fire.

Similarly, our desires, attachments, and emotions can cause an extreme amount of damage if we allow them to control our lives.

You must control the destruction. When this card shows up in a reading, it is time for extreme caution and discipline.

Destruction
Eight of Vajras

Nine of Vajras: Protection

Tarot Archetype: Nine of Swords
(Defense, Readiness)

The lantern protects the fire from that which would extinguish it, while protecting the world from the danger of an uncontrolled flame. It is a safe way to harness the light of the flame.

How can you harness your power to bring benefit? While nothing in this realm of samsara can ever be truly "safe," in Her role as rescuer Tara offers protection to all who call out to Her.

However, be aware that sometimes you need protection from your own desires.

Protection
Nine of Vajras

Ten of Vajras: Magnetism

Tarot Archetype: Ten of Swords
(Oppression, Burdens)

Like attracts like. This is the fundamental principle of magnetism. Each of us has all of the qualities of the Bodhissattvas and Buddhas within us.

The power of magnetism allows us to draw those qualities out of each other.

This radiant sunset creates a magnetic scene, drawing the focus in to a deeper level of understanding. What is drawing you in? What is magnetic to you right now?

You won't be able to avoid it, and if you try it could overwhelm you. Don't allow it to be an oppressive burden. Rather, focus and concentrate. Find the power that is waiting for you.

"Thousands of candles can be lighted from a single candle, and the life of the candle will not be shortened. Happiness never decreases by being shared."- Shakyamuni Buddha[1]

Conclusion: Finding the Wisdom Within

We each have inside of us all of the qualities of the Buddhas and Bodhisattvas. Divine Mother Tara leads us on a fool's journey, and we answer the call.

As we journey through the archetypes of the major arcana, we take her many faces and forms. Like thousands of rainbows reflecting through the faceted prism, we are many and we are one.

We are given many tools along that journey. Some are weapons, intended to forcefully cut through illusions and obstacles. Others are tools of meditation and good fortune.

We sit at peace, offering teachings to those who would hear. We sit with one leg outstretched, willing to go to all who need us. We stand and dance and trample, magnetic and fierce.

We are born of the lotus and surrounded by a halo of moon or sun. Our crown represents our highest mind, while our long hair represents our freedom.

We are the protectors for all who call out to us. We tame the fears and the greatest dangers – the snares and entrapments of the mind.

As dancing dakinis, we offer the eight auspicious symbols of great fortune as an act of devotion. Our prayers are heard.

Through the gold wheels of the Earth, constantly spinning and at rest, we manifest our abundance.

The green bells of wisdom call us to act in accord.

Our blue vases of compassion overflow as we offer benefit to all beings.

And with red lightning vajras, we create a powerful force for good.

Whatever wisdom, compassion, and power we manifest through this sincere practice, may it be for the benefit of all.

Bio of Jessica Zebrine Gray

Jessica Zebrine Gray has been studying with Prema Dasara and practicing Tara mantras, dances, and visualizations since 1997. She took refuge from His Holiness the Karmapa while on pilgrimage to India and Nepal in 2001.

She has danced for and received teachings from many respected Tibetan teachers. She currently serves on the Council of Trustees for the international sacred dance organization Tara Dhatu and has for nearly twenty years.

Zebrine completed her PhD in theatre at Louisiana State University, and she has authored articles about pop culture and performance studies in several books and journals. She runs a theatre-based summer camp and published her first novel, *Imagine the Key* and a collection of plays called *Dramatic Wizardry*, under the pen name Iris Imaginoria.

As a third-level teacher of the Mandala Dance of the 21 Praises of Tara, she shares dharma, dance, and divination in workshops across the country. She also offers Tara Wisdom Card readings via webcam, phone, and in person. Zebrine currently lives in New England with her husband and her teen child.

Bio of Prema Dasara

Prema Dasara is the founder of Tara Dhatu. Using the vehicles of sacred song and dance, Prema has traveled throughout the world in dedicated service to humanity. Her purpose has been to inspire and uplift, inviting everyone to experience the power of their own human potential through sacred music and dance.

Participants in her workshops benefit from her many years of study and practice on the spiritual path. Her joy, exuberance, and friendliness draw everyone who work with her into heartful participation.

She spent six years in India studying the Odissi style of Classical Indian Temple Dance, along with Classical Indian Music, and Sanskrit to deepen her understanding of the Hindu Culture. In 1983 she settled in Hawaii where she became a student of the Tibetan Buddhist meditation master, Lama Sonam Tenzin. He encouraged her to continue her sacred dance work which culminated in the creation of the Mandala Dance of the 21 Praises of Tara, a group ritual based on the profound mind training practices of Tibetan Buddhism.

She has traveled the world since 1986 teaching this dance and the accompanying meditations. She has been invited to present the ritual to many of the most accomplished Tibetan Lamas including His Holiness the Dalai Lama who proclaimed the dance, "wonderful".

Prema teaches with humor and clarity. She leads anyone who participates in her work into an experience of their own potential, and teaches simple, clear methods of developing this wisdom in their day to day life.

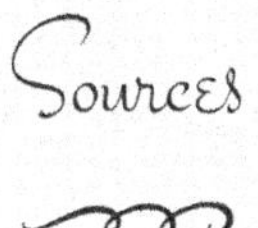

Sources

Primary Sources

Beer, Robert. *The Handbook of Tibetan Buddhist Symbols.* Shambala, 2003.

Beyer, Stephan. *The Cult of Tara: Magic and Ritual in Tibet.* Berkeley: University of CA Press, 1978.

Dasara, Prema. *Dancing Tara: A Manual for Practice.* Tara Dhatu, 2010.

Rinpoche, Bokar. *Tara: The Feminine Divine.* Clearpoint Press, 1999.

Santiago, J.R. *Sacred Symbols of Buddhism.* Pilgrim's Publishing, 2002.

Smith, Pamela Colman and Arthur Edward Waite. *Rider-Waite Tarot Deck.* U.S. Games, 1909.

Background Images

The photographs in the background images are from Flickr's Creative Commons Archive. The photographers who posted these photos gave licensing rights, including publication and derivation, as long as attribution is provided.

Major Arcana

Tara 0 – Rainbow on Ben Nevis by Alex Dixon

Tara 1 – Lightning Over Maidstone, Kent by Carl Revell

Tara 2 – Orion Nebula posted by Paul T, credited to NASA, Hubble Space Telescope.

Tara 3 – Wheat by Jon Bunting

Tara 4 – Smrk mountain by Beskydy

Tara 5 – Shirahama Ohama Beach Sunrise by Izu navi

Tara 6 – Unha rosa para Rosalía by Dani_vr

Tara 7 – Hopewell Scenery-HDR by Nicolas Raymond (www.freestock.ca)

Tara 8 – God is here? by f/orme Pet Photography

Tara 9 – Early-Morning Hike (1) By Nicholas A. Tonelli

Tara 10 - Hurricane Irene Captured August 24, 2011 by NASA Goddard Space Flight Center

Tara 11 - the big storm 2... by Neil Piddock

Tara 12 - Hösten i Botaniska Trädgården by Nahid Vafaie

Tara 13 - Volcanic Eruption by Maxwell Hamilton

Tara 14 – cracked earth2 posted by CIAT, photo by Neil Palmer

Tara 15 – Santa Rosa Island by Robert S. Donovan

Tara 16 - Tornado with dust and debris cloud forming at surface by NOAA Photo Library, NOAA Central Library; OAR/ERL/National Severe Storms Laboratory (NSSL)

Tara 17 – Celebration of Light 2014 - July 26 USA by GoToVan

Tara 18 – Peacock by Madison Berndt

Tara 19 – Waterfall by Oleh Slobodeniuk

Tara 20 – Comet PANNSTARS and the moon above Adelanto by Raymond Shobe

Tara 21 – M31, the Andromeda Galaxy, and M32 and M110 on September 20th, 2014 by Joel Tonyan

Minor Arcana

Rejoicing Tames the Snakes of Jealousy – Snake by Steve Lodefink and snake-cobra--Naja sp. By ASIM CHAUDHURI

Forgiveness Tames the Fires of Anger – Fire by Pure_Nutter and Light it Up by Jason Dirks

Equanimity Tames the Waves of Desire - The little arch wave, Mazatlan, Mexico, Pacific West Coast, North America By Wonderlane and Angry waves at Bluff Beach Iluka by Graham Cook

Generosity Tames the Prison of Greed – Prison Shades and Texturesby Bob Jagendorf and Union by Carla Arenas

Mindfulness Tames the Elephants of Ignorance - Parque Zoológico de São Paulo / Sao Paulo Zoo - Elefante Africano / African Elephant by Deni Williams and Mad Elephant by Justin Hall

Humility Tames the Lions of Pride – Lion – Whipsnade Zoo by Airwolfhound and Roaring Lion by Tambako The Jaguar

Genuineness Tames the Thieves of Wrong Ideas - White face monkey at Palo Verde-1 by John Trainor

Awareness Tames the Demons of Doubt – Upsala Glacier Up Close by David and Question Mark by Konrad Förstner

Parasol of Protection – Sunrise by David Biesack

Fish of Freedom – Under Water by Tonya

Vase of Treasure – Ripples by Crowbared

Pure Lotus – originality by mederndepe

Conch of Sound - Aurora Borealis - Bear Lake, Alaska by Jim Trodel

Knot of Connection – Dew (Explored) by Darren Johnson

Banner of Victory – Toronto by Robert Lowe

Wheel of Truth – Cave Texture Cave Room by paurian

Earth - Wheels

Ace of Wheels - Manifestation – Goodnight Flowers by brillianthues

Two of Wheels - Duality - Zebra, Kruger Park, South Africa by Dimitri B.

Three of Wheels - Diligence The Burning Dhaulagiri by Neil Young

Four of Wheels - Attachment - Favorite Citrine Macro, Large Vug by cobalt123

Five of Wheels – Affliction - Pebbles by C.P. Storm

Six of Wheels - Benefit - Φρούτα, τα εξαιρετικά μέσα για την αποτοξίνωση του σώματος by kanenas.net

Seven of Wheels - Patience - Tree by Henry Burrows

Eight of Wheels - Impermanence - Wisconsin - September 2010 by Nan Palermo

Nine of Wheels - Increase - Sunbeams Streaming through Leaves by Yoshikazu TAKADA

Ten of Wheels - Mastery - San_Juan_Mountains_aspens_Ridgway_CO by Jeff Foster

Air - Bells

Ace of Bells - Wisdom - Athene cunicularia - burrowing owl by Eddie Van 3000

Two of Bells -Balance – Butterfly in Blue by Ray Ashley

Three of Bells – Fears - Himmel över Åkerby 3 by Birger Erikkson

Four of Bells - Refuge – Sun breaking through clouds by Alan Wu

Five of Bells - Dangers - Himmel över Åkerby 3 by Birger Erikkson

Six of Bells - Concentration – Sand Mandala by San Jose Library.

Seven of Bells – Mystery – Fog and wind... going through the trees by Balasubramanya H.R.

Eight of Bells - Freedom - Flyby by Les Chatfield

Nine of Bells – Illusion - DSC07269 by Charles Kremelak

Ten of Bells – Emptiness – The Skies and Beyond by Mendhak

Water - Vases

Ace of Vases - Compassion - Ripples by Sooraj Shajahan

Two of Vases - Connection – Bridge over Pole Cat Creek by Lane Pearman

Three of Vases – Becoming – Raging Waters in Christmasland by Greg Westfall

Four of Vases - Offerings - Waterfall, Mount Baranduda by Dirkus

Five of Vases - Suffering – Stormy Waves by Andrew Bennett

Six of Vases - Remembrance – Waves at Dawn by Jan Smith

Seven of Vases - Creativity - Coral Reef at Palmyra Atoll National Wildlife Refuge by USFWS - Pacific Region

Eight of Vases - Devotion - P1030404 by ctj71081

Nine of Vases – Reflection - Stitched shot of Mt. Rainier reflected on Bench Lake by Frank Kovalchek

Ten of Vases - Fulfillment - Lotus by Scott Akerman

Fire - Vajras

Ace of Vajras - Power – DSC_0065 by Ted

Two of Vajras - Alliance – Double Sun by aneye4wonder

Three of Vajras - Will – Three is a Magic Number by Alan Levine

Four of Vajras – Completion - Sunset Öresund by Håkan Dahlström

Five of Vajras – Obstacles – Fire by Margaret Hoseman

Six of Vajras - Empowerment – Sun between ice by Acid Pix

Seven of Vajras - Confidence – Bearded Dragon... You Looking at Me? By Haydyn Bromley

Eight of Vajras - Destruction - 89 Mesa Fire, 5/6/10 by Coconino National Forest

Nine of Vajras - Protection – The Street Lantern by Tobias Lindman

Ten of Vajras- Magnetism – Another backyard sunset by Rob Baird

Also by Jessica Zebrine

"May There Be Good Fortune" - the song inspired by the offering Goddesses, written by Jessica Zebrine and her husband, Christopher Allen, available on Prema's website of taradhatu.org

A wealth of information and resources about the Tara Mandala dance is available on this website.

Coming soon!

New resources including a new "Tara Tames the Eight Fears Activity Book" for adults.

A special, limited edition version of the Tara Wisdom Cards - available only on Etsy.

Find the most up to date info about the Tara Wisdom Cards on www.tarawisdomcards.com

Make sure you leave us a review wherever you bought the book!

Acknowledgments

Thank you to my Kickstarter backers. Without you, the Tara Wisdom Cards would not exist:

Adrianne LaBry Smith
Aimee Brodeur Johnson
Alexandra Bailey
Amy Hale
Anjali
Barbara T. Gach
Beatriz Giraldo
Beth Ann Townsend
Cynthia, David Perry
David Pollard
Deb Chandy
Deborah Parker
Eana Rose
Elena Sofia Zambrano
Elizabeth Gergaud
Emerson Pirot
Gail M. Syring
Genevra Thurman
Hope
Jacquelyn Sendak
Jeanette Ruyle
Jennifer Cariadus
Jenny Xie

Jocelyn Christy Wolfe
John Opsopaus
Joni Haug
Julie Manning
Karen Nelson Villanueva
Karen Weiss
Kathryn Henderson
Kathryn Morgan
Kathryn ParamGian
Kim Abbey
Kul and Judy Thapa
Kylie Slavik
Laura Lois Greenwood
Layla Centorrino
Lilliha Herington
Linda Davenport
Love Aloha
Lydia Stagg
Maggi Joseph
Mansur Kreps
Maria Antilla
Mary Isabella Stone
Mary Sakara
Michelle Nur Allah Shiloh
Nancy Stewart
Nita Penfold
Patience Harvey
Phyllis Moses
Pia Hagan
Rebecca Reeves
Rev. Michelle Buhite
Rosejayada
Sally G. Jones

Scott & Renee Dumont
Shanti MoonSong Huebner
Sherry Harris
Sofree Roots
Suzanne Chambliss
Suzanne McAnna
Thalassa
The Sowers Family
Therese Spacov
Victoria Scarlett
Vivian Fulk
Wendy Heckscher
Wordsmith
Yeshe Rabbit
Zenia Machado

1. MAJOR ARCANA: THE 21 PRAISES OF TARA

1. Images of Rider-Waite deck are in public domain.

25. COURT CARDS - TARA TAMES THE EIGHT FEARS

1. Dasara, Prema. *Wind Horses: Dharma Songs for Children and the Young at Heart*. Tara Dhatu, no date listed. 6-20.

34. COURT CARDS - AUSPICIOUS OFFERING GODDESSES

1. Beyer, Robert. *The Cult of Tara*. University of CA, 1978. 154-156.

35. THE GODDESS OFFERS THE KNOT OF CONNECTION

1. Dagyab Rinpoche. *Buddhist Symbols*. Somerville, MA: Wisdom Publications, 1995. 25.

36. THE GODDESS OFFERS THE WHEEL OF TRUTH

1. Dagyab Rinpoche 31.

38. THE GODDESS OFFERS THE BANNER OF VICTORY

1. Dagyab Rinpoche 28.

40. THE GODDESS OFFERS THE VASE OF TREASURE

1. Dagyab Rinpoche 22.

41. THE GODDESS OFFERS THE CONCH OF SOUND

1. Dagyab Rinpoche 24.

55. TEN OF WHEELS: MASTERY

1. Buddha. BrainyQuote.com, Xplore Inc, 2016. http://www.brainyquote.com/quotes/quotes/b/buddha118789.html, accessed April 5, 2016.

65. NINE OF BELLS: ILLUSION

1. Joni Mitchell. Both Sides, Now lyrics © Crazy Crow Music / Siquomb Music Publishing, Reservoir Media Management Inc, Songtrust Ave

66. TEN OF BELLS: EMPTINESS

1. Buddha. BrainyQuote.com, Xplore Inc, 2016. http://www.brainyquote.com/quotes/quotes/b/buddha118245.html, accessed April 5, 2016.

77. TEN OF VASES: FULFILLMENT

1. Buddha. BrainyQuote.com, Xplore Inc, 2016. http://www.brainyquote.com/quotes/quotes/b/buddha132910.html, accessed April 5, 2016.

88. TEN OF VAJRAS: MAGNETISM

1. Buddha. BrainyQuote.com, Xplore Inc, 2016. http://www.brainyquote.com/quotes/quotes/b/buddha417367.html, accessed April 5, 2016.

Made in the USA
Middletown, DE
27 April 2024

53548610R00150